W9-BJQ-544

An *essential* study-skills guidebook!

The SECRETS

of

Getting Better Grades

Study Smarter, Not Harder!

Second Edition

Brian Marshall

Park Avenue

The Secrets of Getting Better Grades, Second Edition

© 2002 by JIST Publishing, Inc.

Published by Park Avenue, an imprint of JIST Publishing, Inc.
8902 Otis Avenue
Indianapolis, IN 46216-1033
Phone: 1-800-648-JIST   Fax: 1-800-JIST-FAX   E-mail: info@jist.com

Visit our Web site at **www.jist.com** for information on JIST, free job search information, book chapters, and ordering information on our many products!

See the back of this book for additional JIST titles and ordering information. Quantity discounts are available for JIST books. Please call our Sales Department at 1-800-648-5478 for a free catalog and more information.

Acquisitions and Development Editor: Lori Cates Hand
Contributing Editors: Wendy Ford, Greg Oles, Tony Wright, Jane Newborn, Mary Ellen Stephenson
Interior Designer: Aleata Howard
Page Layout Coordinator: Carolyn J. Newland
Cover Designer: Nick Anderson
Proofreader: Jeanne Clark
Indexer: Larry Sweazy

Printed in the United States of America
06 05 04 03 02   9 8 7 6 5 4 3 2 1

Library of Congress Cataloging-in-Publication data is on file with the Library of Congress.

ISBN 1-57112-112-9

About This Book

Getting good grades is a symbol of achievements…a source of pride…a mark of excellence. For many students, it's a ticket to college and high-paying jobs.

Sadly, most students aren't taught how to study. No one shows them exactly what to do to get good grades. We wrote this book for those students. We wrote this book for you.

In these pages, you'll find almost everything you need to know to succeed in school. You'll discover a system that works like magic. Like magic, it's easy when you know the secrets.

In simple terms, we present what psychologists and educators know about how people think and learn—not all the theory, just what it means in action. We help you translate that into the quickest, easiest ways you can earn top grades in any class.

We hope you want more from your schooling than you're getting right now. Because if you do, you have what it takes to succeed. You're ready to learn and use the secrets in this book.

Contents

About This Book iii

Introduction: Why You Should Read This Book 1

Who Should Read This Book? 1

Who Can Get Good Grades? 1

Why Would You Want Better Grades? 2

What Are the Secrets of Getting Better Grades? 2

    Do These Secrets Actually Work? 2

    Will You Be Able to Understand This System? 3

How to Use This Book 3

How Can You Get the Most Out of This Book? 3

**Chapter 1: Attitude and Time Management: Two Keys
to Better Grades** 5

Challenge Your Attitude 6

    Are You Worth It? 8

    Using Visualization 8

Time Management 9

    Map Out a Schedule 10

    Set an Investment Goal 12

    Follow Your Daily Plan 15

    Planning Tips 16

Quiz 19

**Chapter 2: Learning and Studying by Working
with Your Brain (Not Against It)** 21

Learn How You Learn 23

Use It or Lose It 25

Seven Ways to Make Studying More Effective 27

    A Place for Mind Work 28

    Set Study Times 29

Concentrate 29

Break It Up 30

Mix It Up 30

Food for Thought 31

The Life Connection 31

Start New Habits 32

Quiz 34

Chapter 3: Listening and Taking Notes in Class 37

Be a Class Act 37

Develop Good Listening Habits 40

Prepare to Listen 41

Actively Listen 42

Keep a Record 42

Take Good Notes 43

Master the Mechanics 43

Capture the Essence 51

Attend Every Class 54

Quiz 56

Chapter 4: Read with a Purpose 59

Evaluate the Reason for Your Reading 59

Enter Your Reading Zone 61

Preview the Text Before You Read It 61

Establish the Purpose of the Reading 62

Look for the Structure 62

Form Questions, Guess the Answers 64

Read Actively 65

Reading Mathematics Assignments 66

Speed Reading: Is It for You? 67

Review for Recall 70

Quiz 73

Chapter 5: Writing Papers and Presenting Oral Reports 75

Plan for Excellence 75

Come to Terms with Term Papers 79

Pick a Do-able Topic 79

Evaluate Source Materials 80

Prepare Source Cards 81

Draft the Basic Structure 82

Research and Record 82

Draft a Detailed Outline 83

Now, Write! 83

Read for Meaning 84

Read for Style 84

Prepare the Final Version 85

Conquer Oral Reports and Speeches 85

Connect with the Audience 86

Show and Tell 86

Leave Time for Practice 86

Stand and Deliver 87

Quiz 89

Chapter 6: Review and Memorize What You've Learned 91

Review What You've Learned and Make it Your Own 92

Organize It 92

Sense It 93

Connect It 93

Absorb It 93

See It, Say It 94

Practice It 95

Live It 95

Ask It 95

Keep at It 95

Refresh It 95

Use Super Memory Tricks to Recall Details for Tests 96

    Brain Cartoons 97

    Stroll Down Memory Lane 98

    Eight on the Garden Gate 99

    Creative Acronyms and Sentences 100

    Rhyming Verses 101

    Rhythm and Beat 101

    Number Games 101

Study Wisely for Tests 103

Quiz 106

Chapter 7: Tackle Tests with Confidence 109

Know the Testing Techniques 109

    True/False 111

    Multiple Choice 111

    Matching 112

    Short Answer, Fill in the Blanks 112

    Story Problems 113

    Discussion or Essay Questions 114

Develop Good Test-Taking Habits 117

    Have a Plan of Attack 118

    Review Your Results 121

    Learn from Your Mistakes 121

Quiz 124

Chapter 8: Go For It! 129

Make Our Secrets Your Secrets 129

Put Your Tool Kit to Work 130

    Using the Tools in Other Courses 131

    Using the Tools for Other Reasons 132

Write Your Own Story 132

Program Yourself to Succeed 133

Savor Your Successes 134

Quiz 135

Appendix: Web Sites for Getting Better Grades **137**

Study Skills Web Sites 138

Web Sites About School Subjects 139

Book Summaries on the Web 141

Online Reference Resources and Tools............................ 141

Search Engines for Further Research 143

Glossary **145**

Index.. **147**

© Park Avenue, an imprint of JIST Publishing, Inc.

Why You Should Read This Book

Schoolwork doesn't have to be hard! Many students make it harder than it needs to be. They see education as a chore. They spend their school time being resentful, confused, and afraid. Could this be you?

You can make your schoolwork easier by working smarter, not harder. This book shows you how.

Who Should Read This Book?

Are you a top student? Are you confident when you go into a test? Do you have a strong memory? Do you feel good about yourself and your future? If you hesitate to answer "yes" to any of these questions, this book is for you. We wrote it for anyone who is ready to learn a step-by-step recipe for success.

Who Can Get Good Grades?

You can! If you apply what you learn in these pages, you can get better grades. The more you apply these techniques, the more your grades will improve. You don't have to be a genius. You don't have to love school. You don't have to be the teacher's favorite student. You just need to follow a few simple instructions.

Why Would You Want Better Grades?

You may need good grades to win a scholarship. (Even people who get athletic scholarships need good grades if they expect to play!) You may want good grades because they show you've learned something, or because they stand for success. Your school may require you to maintain a certain grade-point average to be eligible to participate in extracurricular activities such as sports and school dances. You may want good grades to land a high-paying job, increase your self-confidence, or get into a better college.

Whatever your reasons, the habits that make you a top student will serve you all your life. Good learning skills are also success skills.

What Are the Secrets of Getting Better Grades?

The first secret of getting better grades is to have a system. The best system is one that tells you what to do every step of the way. That's what this book will show you. Think of it as a toolkit for building better learning habits.

Each chapter shows you step-by-step how to use the tools to make studying easier and get better results. Your task is to use the tools to make schoolwork less boring and more rewarding.

Some tools will work for you, whereas others might not. Use one tool or many; it's up to you. But the more tools you use, and the more you practice with them, the more you will build essential skills for tackling challenges of all kinds.

Do These Secrets Actually Work?

Every technique in this book has been tried and tested in just about every type of class. The tools are based on what scientists know about how we learn and how we can think and work better. The only way to know whether the system works for you is to try it. Only then will you see the results. You'll see how easy it can be to study, learn, and earn good grades.

Will You Be Able to Understand This System?

We'll make sure you do, by breaking up each technique into simple steps. For example, here's a simple way to look at school. It's made up of two parts:

1. What you do inside the classroom.

2. What you do outside the classroom.

Inside the classroom, you listen to the teacher, look at visual aids, discuss with other students, recite to the teacher, compute, handle equipment, and take notes. Outside the classroom, you read textbooks, work problems, prepare reports, and study for tests. Maybe no one has ever taught you the basics of doing these tasks. This book teaches you better ways to do them.

How to Use This Book

You can pick it up and start reading anywhere. Each chapter has tips and techniques that you'll find useful. Be sure to read all the chapters to get the complete toolkit.

Each chapter includes examples, pictures, exercises, and quizzes to help you learn and remember the material. It also includes special features to help you relate the tools to your own experience:

? Questions about how you're doing things now

🕐 Tips on how to better manage your time

A⁺ Quizzes on what you've read

📝 Plans to take advantage of what you learn in each chapter

How Can You Get the Most Out of This Book?

Make it real by picking one subject in which you would like to do better. Is it math, science, history, English, or a foreign language? Decide to try one or more of the tools that you learn in this book. Apply them to this subject in class and outside of class. Watch what happens to your grades and your confidence. Then try those tools in other subjects.

After you finish reading this book, scan it again from time to time to review the main ideas. This will keep your study skills sharp. You'll also get new ideas of how to use the tools each time you read about them.

Things to Think About

Before you begin, think about your answers to the following questions:

1. What is your biggest motivation for wanting to get better grades?

2. Pick a subject in which you would like to improve your grade.

3. How do you hope this book will help you improve in your chosen subject?

4. What else do you want to get out of this book?

CHAPTER 1

Attitude and Time Management: Two Keys to Better Grades

Does life happen to you? Or do you make it happen? It may seem as though everything is controlling your life for you—school, your parents, your part-time job, your finances (or lack of them). But whether you realize it or not, you make choices every day that determine what happens to you.

This chapter shows you how to do the following:

- Take control of your attitude through what you tell yourself about you.

- Take control of how you spend your time.

These are two choices you can make every day to help yourself get better grades. If you can first master your attitude and your time, everything else will fall into place.

Challenge Your Attitude

Your mind is a powerful thing. It has the power to think, feel, and direct your actions. It experiences the outside world through touch, movement, sight, smell, hearing, and taste, and tries to make sense of it. But it also comes under the influence of *self-talk*. Self-talk has a lot of power, too.

Let's say you sit down to take a math test. You have studied carefully but still feel a little unsure of yourself. You do the first few problems with ease. Then you stumble over the fifth problem. A little voice starts up in your head: "Tsk, tsk. You blew that one. Boy, you sure are dumb. You never were any good with numbers. You'll never get to college. You'll still be working at McDonald's when you're 50."

That inner voice is like a reporter at a news event, putting a "spin" on what just happened. In this case, it's bad news, so your body responds the way it does to anything frightening: Your palms sweat; your stomach churns; you begin to panic. Your mind leaps out of your seat and runs for a safer place.

Suppose you rewrite the script for that inner voice. You've stumbled over the fifth problem. Your inner voice pipes up: "Hmm, that problem is worded funny. I bet you can puzzle it out if you relax. After all, you are a good student, and you prepared for this test. You have what it takes to figure it out."

Does your own inner voice predict doom and gloom for the hometown fans? Or does it urge you to cheer for the courageous home team? Introduce yourself to that little voice. Tell it that you don't want to hear any discouraging words. You want to find silver linings in all clouds.

If you tell yourself good things about you, you come to believe them—and your actions will reflect what you believe. In turn, your actions convince others of your "smarts," and they will reward your positive attitude by treating you as a smart student.

Try On an Attitude

Do you ever listen to yourself think about your abilities? What does that little voice in your mind say? Check off all of the following statements that sound like you:

- It's not my fault that I'm getting a *C* in chemistry. The teacher just doesn't explain things right.
- School doesn't let me use any of my real talents.
- School's not all fun and games, but I study when I need to and pass my tests with flying colors.
- I get so bored with classes that I can hardly stand it. I'd rather be out on the soccer field scoring a winning goal.
- I look forward to reading my textbook, even though it's pretty dull. I feel so good when I'm done.
- I like English but hate math. I break out in a cold sweat just thinking about algebra.
- I hate to read. Books and I just don't get along.
- I'll never learn Spanish, no matter how hard I try.
- I'm a poor student, so I might as well accept it. Besides, I'm never going to amount to anything, so why go to the trouble of studying?
- That teacher is out to get me.
- My friends will think I'm weird if I get *A*s on tests.
- I didn't get an *A* on that test, but I'll keep trying no matter what. I'm not a quitter.
- I'll never get this paper written on time.
- I will earn an academic scholarship to the university.
- Math is not useful for what I want to do in life.
- Nobody knows who I really am. I'd like to keep it that way.
- I dread presenting an oral report in class.
- If I begin to do better in school, people will expect more of me, and I don't want that pressure.
- There must be something I'm good at. I'm always on the lookout for chances to find out.

(continues)

Try On an Attitude (continued)

○ I don't have a future, so why bother preparing for one?

○ I will be president some day.

Now assume an attitude that is the opposite of yours. Imagine how you would look and act if you had that attitude. Picture yourself being that person. See yourself going to school, talking with friends, answering questions in class, taking a test, spending the after-school hours. Close your eyes and see yourself as that person now.

How does your imagined self act? Do your actions match your new attitude? How does your behavior differ when you use this different attitude?

This is a major secret of getting better grades: **By changing your attitude, you can harness the power of your mind to make your schoolwork (not to mention your life) easier.** Control your self-talk, and you've made a good start toward becoming a top student.

Are You Worth It?

Shifting negative self-talk to positive seems easier said than done. First, you have to believe deep down inside that you're worth it. Tell your little voice that you deserve better than what you now have, and that you're worth it. Keep telling yourself that until you believe it. Say it out loud. Feel how it feels. If you're worth it, you have a reason to develop your abilities and to dream dreams.

Using Visualization

Picture in your mind what you would like to be doing 5 or 10 years from now. Do you have a good job that you enjoy? Are you attending a good college, surrounded by other successful students? Are you sharing your artistic or athletic talent with the community? Successfully running a business? Helping people lead better lives?

Close your eyes and see yourself being successful in what you would like to do. Fill the picture with details. Make it come alive for you. Do it now.

Now keep that vision. It will feed your inner voice with positive messages about where you are going. The more real you can make that vision, the more your self-talk and your actions will fall into line with that thinking. It's a way to program your mind to naturally do things that make your vision become your future.

You can use this technique—which is called *visualization*—with other goals besides a successful life. You can even use it with schoolwork. Your old mental habits may be getting in the way of learning your school subjects. Your power to visualize success helps remove these roadblocks. As for that inner voice, tell it to go easy on you. You need all the support you can get!

Time Management

When life happens to you rather than you taking charge of your life, you feel like a victim all the time. You're the do-ee rather than the do-er. One of the worst offenders for making people feel like victims is time. The clock never stops running, not even to let you catch your breath! But you do have some choices that give you greater control.

It's no accident that we speak of "spending" time. Time is a precious resource. Each of us has a certain allotment, and that's all we have to work with. Once it's gone, it's gone. There's no way to make it up. At best, making up for lost time will cost you later when you have to give up something else you wanted to do.

If you can spend time, you can also invest it. If you invest it, you get something back. It's not just gone and forgotten. Think of time as something to invest in yourself and your vision. To do so, you must choose to take control. You can't control the steady march of time, but you can control how you invest your time. Because you're worth it, you want to invest time in making yourself better and making your vision a reality. Now we'll show you how.

Where Does the Time Go?

How did you spend your time yesterday? How do you plan to spend it today? If you have only a vague idea, try this exercise:

1. Keep track of what you do for a whole day. Every 15 minutes, notice what you are doing and write it on a page in your notebook.

2. Before you go to bed, look over your time log. Next to each 15-minute entry, note whether you did schoolwork, participated in family activities, chatted online, worked on fitness or athletics, had fun with friends, surfed the Web, played Nintendo, worked at a job, or watched TV.

3. What do you notice about the day's activities? Are you satisfied with how you spent your time? What do you wish you had done differently?

Map Out a Schedule

You can get a better handle on the time you have to invest if you map it out. This lets you "see" some distance into the future and lay out a plan for investing your time wisely.

You've probably used a class schedule to keep track of the times you attend various classes. A variation on the class schedule lets you plan your time outside of class as well as inside. You can make your own, buy a "day planner" book such as Premier's discoveragenda, use a computer scheduling program such as Microsoft Outlook, or use a personal digital assistant (PDA) such as Handspring or Palm Pilot.

For now, use the weekly schedule form provided here. Notice that it includes the whole day, from early morning to late at night, and all seven days of the week. Copy the blank form to write on so that you will have a clean one for making additional schedules.

Weekly Schedule

Week of _____

Time	Mon	Tue	Wed	Thur	Fri	Sat	Sun
6:00							
7:00							
8:00							
9:00							
10:00							
11:00							
12:00							
1:00							
2:00							
3:00							
4:00							
5:00							
6:00							
7:00							
8:00							
9:00							
10:00							
11:00							
12:00							

Now here's what to do:

1. Using a pencil, fill in any prescheduled blocks of time, such as classes, meals, jobs, and family chores. Include transportation time. (Be sure to set aside eight or nine hours for a good night's sleep.) You started with about 126 hours (sounds like a lot!). How many hours do you have left to work or play?

Hours Available

2. Now fill in blocks of time for your planned workouts, regular club meetings, choir practice, social activities, and so on. Do you have any time left for studying? Look at the blocks of time you have left to work with.

Study Hours Available

3. Block out any good-sized chunks of time as study time. Don't try to fill up every hour of the day. Instead, look for half-hour to two-hour periods that would round out a morning, afternoon, or evening.

The chart on page 13 shows how your completed schedule might look.

You're almost ready to think about how to invest these hours in schoolwork. But first you need to set some goals.

Set an Investment Goal

A goal—something you'd like to accomplish—will help you decide how to invest those blocks of study time. That's the whole purpose of a goal—to determine what you want to accomplish. The goal is the desired end product. What you do now helps get you there.

Remember that subject you chose in the Introduction as the one in which you'd like a better grade? Why not set a goal for that class? Your goal should meet the following three requirements:

- Your goal should be **measurable,** so that you can tell whether you achieved it.

Weekly Schedule

Week of __November 4__

Time	Mon	Tue	Wed	Thur	Fri	Sat	Sun
6:00	paper route	paper route	paper route	paper route	paper route	paper route	paper route
7:00	shower/ breakfast	shower/ breakfast	shower/ breakfast	shower/ breakfast	shower/ breakfast	shower	shower
8:00	in class	in class	in class	in class	in class	breakfast	breakfast
9:00						study	church
10:00						study	
11:00						study	study
12:00						lunch	study
1:00						study	dinner
2:00						basket- ball	visit grandma
3:00	↓	↓	↓	↓	↓		go for walk
4:00	band	study	band	study	band	clean room	study
5:00	study	go for walk	study	study	study	TV	
6:00	supper	supper	supper	supper	supper	supper	
7:00	study	TV	study	TV	family game night	go out with friends	supper
8:00	TV	study	study	TV			take out trash
9:00	study	study	TV	listen to music			
10:00	sleep	sleep	sleep	sleep	sleep	↓	sleep
11:00						sleep	
12:00	↓	↓	↓	↓	↓	↓	↓

- It should be **realistic**, something you can reasonably do. If you set your goals too high at first, it will be difficult to meet them and you will feel discouraged. So think carefully about what you can reasonably expect of yourself. As you get better at this system, you can increase your expectations.

- Your goal must also **have a deadline** so that you'll know when you need to accomplish it.

Here are some examples of goals you might set:

- To neatly complete my math homework each night before it's due, for a whole week.

- Complete my English paper in two weeks.

- Review my physics notes within 24 hours of each class for the next 10 classes.

- Keep up with assigned reading for American history for a whole week.

- Prepare a detailed outline for a 10-minute oral report by a week from Friday.

- Read Dickens's *Great Expectations* by December 15th.

- By Monday, learn the 15 new French words in chapter 6 and be able to use each of them in a sentence.

After you've set a goal, you can decide how to use your time. Think through everything you have to do to achieve your goal. Write down all the steps.

Here's an example. Say your goal was to read *Great Expectations* by December 15, and today is December 1.

1. Look at the book and see how long it is. In this case, it's 59 chapters (but they're short!).

2. Figure out how many days you have to get the reading done. In this case, it's 15 days.

3. Divide the number of chapters you need to read by the number of days you have. The result is about four chapters a day.

4. Figure out how long it will take you to read four chapters. Maybe an hour is plenty of time.

5. Look at your weekly schedule and try to find an hour of available study time each day to set aside for reading. If one day has no available time, set aside two hours on another day (maybe during the weekend) to make up for it.

6. By December 15, you will have finished reading the book!

Now you have an investment plan. If you follow it, you'll have a nice payoff when you achieve your goal!

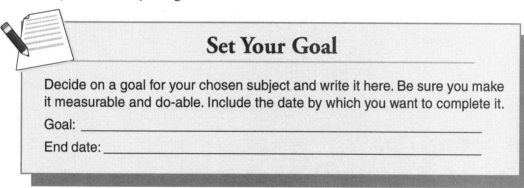

Set Your Goal

Decide on a goal for your chosen subject and write it here. Be sure you make it measurable and do-able. Include the date by which you want to complete it.

Goal: _____

End date: _____

Follow Your Daily Plan

Lots can go wrong between the time you make your plan and the deadline: family fun, TV shows, naps, phone calls, talkative friends, offers you can't refuse, and so on. You need a system to help you follow your plan.

Before your day starts, take a look at what you have scheduled for that day. You need to set some priorities to help organize your time. This will take no more than 5 or 10 minutes, and it's time well invested. It will move you steadily toward your goal.

Here's how to plan your day:

1. On a separate sheet, list all the things you want to get done that day. Include any time that you have planned for the steps toward your goal. Also include errands, exercise, and chores you need to do.

2. Now look at each item and decide how important it is. Does it have to be done today? If so, mark it with an *A*. Can it wait a few days? Mark it with a *B*.

3. Look at all the items marked with an *A*. Which is the most important? Mark it *A1*. Which is the next most important? Mark it *A2*. Do this with all the *A*s. Then do the same thing with the *B*s.

4. Now you have your marching orders for the day. Get the *A*s done for sure. Block out time on your schedule to get them done. Remember that *A1* takes priority over *A5*. Also schedule any of the *B*s that you have time for.

When you get the hang of this, it's easy to do. Try it for two weeks. We bet you'll get an idea of how to invest your time to achieve your goals.

Planning Tips

- Do your planning in pencil. We guarantee you'll need to make adjustments. Your weekly schedule and daily priority list are tools, not slave-drivers. Think of them as gentle reminders of how you plan to get where you're going.

- Don't try to schedule every minute of the day. You need breathing space between activities to just relax and enjoy life. You also need to figure in extra time as a "fudge factor," so that your schedule doesn't fall apart if an activity runs longer than you planned.

- A good time to plan your day is the night before. Your memory of what still needs to be done is more fresh at that time than it will be the next morning when you're still sleepy. With a plan in your head, you can leap out of bed in the morning and tackle the world.

We'll talk more about goals and planning in later chapters. You can use these techniques to make school easier. You'll find they make your life easier, too. Remember, you're worth it, so take control of your precious time and make it work for you.

Make a Commitment to This System

Set another goal—to use this time control system for as long as needed to reach the goal for your chosen subject. State this goal in your own words.

_____

_____

_____

Rudy

Rudy groaned as the teacher handed back his English test. Another *C*. "Who cares about Hamlet and his weird girlfriend anyway," he muttered, pitching the test paper in the trash as he headed for the door. "That's old stuff, and it's the twenty-first century—who needs it!"

Rudy hadn't done half of his assignments in English, and he barely cracked the book for Shakespeare. But he wasn't thinking about *why* he got a *C* on the test when he slammed his books down on the table in study hall. He spent the next 15 minutes badmouthing the English teacher for assigning too much homework. He was sick and tired of writing essays, reading short stories, and comparing and contrasting this and that author and this and that literary work. He had better things to do, after all…. Then he drifted off into his favorite daydream, seeing himself masterminding all the special effects at a major rock concert.

Rudy was jolted out of his reverie when he realized the other students were leaving for the next class. Darn, he hadn't even started on his chemistry assignment. "Oh well, who needs chemistry anyway," he thought. "Looks like another rotten school year for me."

After an after-school pickup game of basketball at home with his friends, he brushed by his sister who said, "You're in big trouble now, Rudy. You were supposed to empty the trash." "The world's out to get me today, it seems,"

(continues)

(continued)

thought Rudy. He raced up to his room where he could be what he loved to be: a sound engineer. Donning his headphones, he cranked up the special-effects machine and the CD player. Music filled his head and Rudy came alive, delicately adjusting the knobs and levers to get just the right sounds. Late into the night he twirled dials, programmed the drum machine, and played guitar licks in all different combinations and permutations of sound. As his head hit the pillow, his thoughts were far from Shakespeare and chemistry and French. "Oh darn! French! I forgot I have a test in French tomorrow."

That night a big storm came up, and thunder and lightning kept Rudy tossing and turning until the wee hours of the morning. It wasn't just the storm keeping him awake. Things weren't going so well for Rudy. He was unhappy with his life and the direction it was taking. He did a lot of thinking that night. As the birds began their morning songfest, Rudy sat up in bed and had a little chat with himself. "If you're going to go to college and get your degree so you can be a sound engineer, Rudy, you're going to have to clean up your act. It's time to take control!"

The first thing Rudy did that morning was write a note and paste it on his mirror. "I'm in charge," it said. During his free period he drew himself a weekly schedule form. He mapped out all his classes, chores, band practice, and the weekly jam session at the music store.

Several nice blocks of time were left in the afternoon and evening. And, of course there was his free period before lunch every day. These were times he usually fiddled with his sound system ideas, Rudy thought sadly. Maybe he would have to invest some of that time in studying now to make his dream really happen. He had daydreamed it long enough to know exactly how great it would be. "I guess it's worth some sacrifice," thought Rudy. "And I'm worth it, too."

"First, I'll tackle English," Rudy thought. It was the class he felt most behind in. I want to get a *B* on the next test, and an *A* on the one after that. He wrote those goals in large letters in his notebook.

The next day a second note appeared on Rudy's mirror: "I keep up with my daily English assignments." Rudy was on his way. He made time every day for reading Shakespeare, writing essays, and comparing and contrasting great works of literature. Every night, he reviewed the next day's schedule and set priorities for the things he wanted to accomplish. English was always *A1* and at the top of the list.

Rudy's mirror was quickly disappearing behind the daily notes: "I invest my time wisely." "I am headed for college to prepare for a successful career in sound engineering." "I am an *A* student in English." Rudy's mood was lifting. He felt better about school than he had for a long time. He was beginning to see results. His sister couldn't believe he even remembered to take out the trash.

One morning three months later, Rudy took down the note that said, "I am an *A* student in English." He didn't need a reminder anymore because he had proof on his test papers. In its place he put a new note: "I am an *A* student in chemistry." He smiled and strode off to tackle the day.

Quiz

1. This chapter was about how to take control of your _____ and your _____.

2. How can a positive vision of your future help you control negative self-talk? _____

   _____

3. Name three requirements for a goal. _____

   _____

   _____

4. Why is it important to set priorities for your daily tasks? _____

   _____

   _____

True or False?

5. Always write your daily plan in ink so that you won't be tempted to change it. T F

6. When planning your day, be certain to schedule every minute so that you won't waste any time. T F

7. The end of the day is an ideal time to plan tomorrow's activities. T F

CHAPTER 2

Learning and Studying by Working *with* Your Brain (Not Against It)

When you get down to it, people are pretty darn smart. Look at babies. They begin life crying and cooing, and in just a few years develop an incredibly rich language. If you're struggling with a foreign language, imagine traveling to that country. You'll see little children all over the place talking that language! If they can do it, you can too.

Their secret is that their brain is programmed to learn a language. Through experiences they have with their parents and through playing with sounds (babbling), they learn to talk in certain patterns: saying what they want, asking a question, giving a command, describing something that happened to them.

Your brain works the same way. It's programmed to recall things that happen, especially if they happen over and over. It's also programmed to see patterns among different things that happen. In time, it builds up complex concepts. It can use those concepts to understand patterns it has never seen before. Pretty talented!

❓ Where Do You Shine?

There are all kinds of "smart." Some of them are listed below. You probably shine in some areas and fade in others. Circle those that you feel are your stronger points. Add to the list any other areas you think of that you're pretty good at.

Music	Numbers	Sensitive to people
Words	Drawing	Athletics
Puzzles	Designing	Dancing
Working independently	Building	Leadership
Common sense	Logical argument	Self-understanding
_____	_____	_____
_____	_____	_____
_____	_____	_____
_____	_____	_____

Now you have a profile of your strengths. What do you think about what you see? Can you develop your strengths to help you do well in school? Can you turn any other areas into strengths by working on them?

This is not a course in brain anatomy, but we'd like to introduce you to your brain and how it works. You can make schoolwork a lot easier if you work with your brain, not against it. Learn its secrets for remembering things, and feed it what it needs to remember your schoolwork. The result: better grades!

Learn How You Learn

Your brain is like a huge, drafty, dusty warehouse. It has several doorways guarded by your senses: sight, hearing, taste, touch, and smell. The only way anything gets into storage is through one or more of these senses. As you move through the world, information goes through these doors all the time. This drafty warehouse is your *subconscious* mind, or your memory bank.

If you're not paying attention, information from the senses gets stored pretty much wherever it lands. However, when you're paying attention, it's like there's a master organizer keeping track of where things get stored. This is your *conscious mind.*

When you're awake and alert, your conscious mind stands by to receive information from the senses. It takes each piece of incoming information and *processes* it—looks at it, turns it over, decides where it fits in, and puts it there with other similar pieces. Things that look, feel, or taste the same go together in neat stacks—important things on the left, unimportant things on the right. Over time, one of the stacks may grow pretty tall. The conscious mind looks it over, takes its measure, paces out a new storage location, gives it a label, rearranges the contents in finer groupings—and voilá, you have a *concept.* That concept helps to make sense out of other new information that comes in.

Your conscious mind is good at storing things in proper order. Luckily, it's also great at taking things out of storage—it *retrieves* information. If it weren't for the conscious mind, everything stored in your memory banks would just sit there and never be used. As the world goes by, your conscious mind evaluates your situation and draws out information to help you make sense of what's going on. It remembers where stuff is stored and goes to retrieve it. Then you can react to what's going on by speaking, moving, running, or focusing your senses on specific events.

Different Kinds of Smart

Psychologist and educator Howard Gardner describes the concept of multiple intelligences. He says people have different amounts of each type of intelligence. What can you learn about your own abilities by studying Gardner's concept?

Intelligence Type	Skill	Likes	Career Use
Linguistic	Good with words	Telling stories, playing with sounds of words	Writer, translator, actor
Logical-Mathematical	Good with reasoning, visual thinking, nonverbal problem solving	Puzzles, logical arguments, computers	Computer analyst, economist, scientist
Spatial	Good at seeing position of objects in space	Drawing, designing, machines, daydreaming	Artist, architect, engineer, pilot, sailor
Body	Has a sense of the body and how it moves in space	Movement	Dancer, actor, athlete, craftsperson
Musical	Good with sounds and rhythms of music	Singing, playing instruments, picky about what he listens to	Musician, dancer
Interpersonal/Social	Understands people and how to deal with them	Being with people, leading people to get things done	Politician, sales specialist, psychologist
Intrapersonal	Knows oneself and one's abilities, able to control own emotions	Having opinions, enjoys working independently	Writer, entrepreneur, psychologist, minister

*Adapted from Howard Gardner, *Frames of Mind: The Theory of Multiple Intelligences.* New York: Basic Books, 1993.

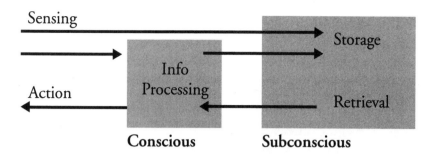

Sensing

Storage

Action

Info Processing

Retrieval

Conscious   Subconscious

Mini-Quiz

What part of your mind processes, stores, and retrieves information?

_____

What is a concept? _____

_____

How does your mind receive information? _____

_____

_____

Use It or Lose It

Have you got the picture? Now, here are some of the finer points about memory:

- Over time, a lot of dust settles on all the stuff stored in your brain. But the conscious mind wears a clear path to the facts you use often. For example, it has no trouble retrieving your best friend's phone number.

  The more often your conscious mind has to store or retrieve a certain fact, the less the dust has a chance to settle. The path to that fact is easier to find. This is the mental version of "use it or lose it."

- When a brand new idea comes in that the conscious mind has never dealt with—like the Pythagorean theorem—it makes a best guess as to where to put it. If you need to retrieve that idea two weeks later, your conscious mind is left scratching its head. Now let's see, where did I put that? Did I put it with famous Greeks, with stuff about triangles, or with names that start with *P*?

If you know you're going to need that idea two weeks from now—say, for the midterm geometry test—ask your conscious mind to haul it out of storage a couple of times between now and then. Your conscious mind gets several chances to wear a path to its location. This works especially well if you ask for the idea soon after you first put it in storage.

- A lot of stuff that comes in from the senses gets past the conscious mind and settles on the warehouse floor with all the rest of the clutter. That stuff is hard to retrieve (hypnotists seem to have a way of getting to it, though). The conscious never had a chance to sort that information into stacks because it wasn't paying attention to it.

What makes your conscious pay attention? All of a sudden a booming voice comes over the warehouse loudspeaker: "Thou shalt watch for ways to use the Pythagorean theorem in the real world." It's The Boss. From then on, your conscious scans all incomings and latches on to those The Boss wants, like a magnet. Nothing even remotely connected to a hypotenuse gets by your conscious mind. The Boss (you, taking charge!) has spoken.

Once in a while, your conscious has to latch on to a big, ugly, confusing topic. It's much too big to fit in the door of just one of the senses. But The Boss wants it, so you cram it in through several different doors: eyes, ears, touch, whatever works. What magnificent teamwork as your senses and your conscious mind drag the big, ugly topic, kicking and screaming, through the doors and arrange its parts neatly in a storage bin alongside other formerly confusing topics!

A wonderful thing happens while you're going about your busy day or sleeping at night. Little elves come out from behind all the piles in the warehouse and take inventory and sift through what's there. They do a little sorting and stacking while you're not even paying attention. Then all of a sudden your conscious mind realizes it's got a new concept, one it wasn't even consciously working on. These little elves are great helpers. Just give them plenty of time and plenty of facts to work with. They can neaten up even the most disorganized storage bins.

Your memory warehouse, your storage and retrieval manager, The Boss, the neat-freak elves—keep these images in mind as you read the rest of this book. They help explain why the secrets of getting better grades really work.

Mini-Quiz

A⁺

Who works in your memory warehouse? _____

What do these workers do? _____

_____

Seven Ways to Make Studying More Effective

Now that you have a picture of your brain, here are ways you can work with your brain, not at cross-purposes.

As you can tell, the brain is searching for order. It tries to organize what it hears, smells, tastes, touches, and sees. It loves habits because it doesn't have to pay so much attention; it just does what it's used to doing. You can make that love of habits work for you or against you, depending on what kind of habits you develop.

Your conscious mind works hard to process all the input from your senses. Even when The Boss says it's time to focus on one particular type of input, your brain may have a hard time focusing if there's too much going on around you. Give it a break by setting the stage for concentration.

"Studying," by the way, can involve many different activities. You might read an assigned chapter about World War II for history class and also possibly answer questions about what you've read. You might have to work several problems for math class. Your science teacher may have asked you to make a chart that diagrams the digestive system of a mammal. Other teachers may have assigned you to complete a worksheet or write an essay.

All of these activities require you to focus and concentrate. The following sections show you how. These simple habits help you make the most of your study time so that you can get it done and go have some fun.

A Place for Mind Work

Find a calm place to study and get in the habit of studying there. Once the habit is set, your brain will automatically settle down when you arrive there. It will prepare to concentrate.

Set up this place so your brain doesn't get interrupted constantly: your body grumbling "too hot," your eyes whining "too dark," your legs jumping up to sharpen a pencil or find your textbook. You especially don't want this place to be linked with another habit, like watching TV or sleeping. (Bed is out! Your brain will prepare itself for sleep, not for study.)

So here's what your ideal "study zone" needs:

- Plenty of light
- An even temperature
- A good chair that you can sit straight in
- Your writing tools, equipment, and books
- Room to spread out your papers
- No food
- No clutter
- No chatty friends
- No leaping pets
- No loud music that you can't resist singing the words to
- Telephone ringer turned off
- No TV

The moment you arrive at this study zone, all the things you see will spell "study time," and your brain will be ready for action.

Your Study Zone

Where do you do your homework? Close your eyes and see yourself doing your homework as usual. Where are you? In what position is your body? What is going on around you? Who or what else is there? Are you concentrating on your studies? How long does your studying last? Get in touch with your study habits. Do this now.

Set Study Times

Try to study about the same time every day. Your brain will get used to it and give you its best shot. If possible, schedule your hardest subjects for times when you feel most energetic, usually at the beginning of your study session. If you leave the hardest subject till last, you're working against your brain, not with it. If you do the hardest thing first, your next study task will feel like a reward.

Concentrate

Work on one task at a time. Give your brain a chance to focus its full attention on what you're trying to do. If you are settling down for some heavy reading, allow time to ease into the reading task (you'll read more on how to do this in chapter 4). It may take 10 to 20 minutes before you reach full concentration. If you have a special place for mind work, your mind will settle down sooner for the task ahead.

 Why Do I Have to Do Homework?

Maybe the last thing you feel like doing after spending a full day in class is to come home and do homework. That's perfectly understandable. But there are many good reasons to do your homework—and to do it correctly and neatly:

1. Homework is a way to expand on what you've learned in class and help reinforce the concepts.

(continues)

Why Do I Have to Do Homework? (continued)

2. Doing homework teaches you self-discipline, responsibility, and independence that will help you throughout your life.

3. The reading and research skills you learn by doing homework will also pay off later.

4. You can look over your corrected homework and use it to figure out where you need to improve before the test.

5. And if you don't care about all the other items on this list, consider this: Most teachers count homework as part of your grade in some way. Skip your homework and your grades will suffer!

Break It Up

Mind work can be intense. If you have two hours of studying to do, don't make it one marathon session. Break it up. Your body and brain need a two-minute break about every 15 minutes. Stand up and stretch and yawn. Take a couple of deep breaths and hold them to feed your brain some extra oxygen. Then go back to work. At the end of 50 minutes, take a real break. Walk to the kitchen, stare out the window, eat a piece of fruit. Then go back to work. Remember, these breaks are not a time to call a friend or get online. Doing these things puts you at risk for losing track of time and possibly wandering away from your studies.

Mix It Up

Plan your study time in blocks that require contrasting skills. If you have a ton of reading to do for government class, mix it up with blocks of math, art, or vocabulary study. Your brain will feel refreshed. That ton of reading will seem like do-able chunks.

Food for Thought

Feed your brain a rich diet of pictures, sounds, movement, and touch. If it has trouble getting an idea through words, draw a picture of the idea. Or pretend you are holding the idea in your hand, turning it over, feeling its weight, and tossing it in the air. You might try reading the text or idea out loud. Use your eyes, ears, nose, fingers, or tongue—whatever helps that idea get through the doors of your memory warehouse.

The Life Connection

Use every chance to apply what you learn to your life outside of school. Every link to your everyday experience gives what you learn more meaning. Your brain gets better organized. It has more storage categories to fit things in, and more ways to make sense of them. You'll soon learn that study skills can be life skills. Make the connection while you're still in school, and see how much easier life can be.

A⁺   Mini-Quiz

Name the seven good study habits: _____

_____

_____

_____

_____

_____

_____

Of the distractions listed in the previous section, which ones exist in the place where you study? _____

_____

_____

_____

Start New Habits

You've been in school almost your whole life, so you already have a set of habits for schoolwork. If you want to get better grades, think about whether those study habits are working with your brain or against it. Do you have some unhelpful habits? Don't just get rid of them; replace them with helpful habits.

Start by deciding what needs to change. Then change your behavior for 21 days. That's how long it takes to start a new habit. Tell your friends and family about the changes you're making and why, so that they become part of the solution and not part of the problem.

Decide to change your habits, and then stick it out. Your brain needs time to adjust to new patterns in the way you do things, but it will adjust. Your brain loves habits, so it will be just as happy with a good habit as a bad one. Give your new habits the time they need to become established. Then you'll have a chance to see for yourself how much easier they make your schoolwork. Invest some time in changing your study habits, and stand by for the payoff.

Which New Study Habits Will You Use?

Which habits will you change to give your brain a fighting chance to help you get better grades? Think about the special subject in which you want to improve your grade. Write down which new study habits you will practice for that class, and for how long. Remember to keep your new goals reasonable and attainable.

_____

_____

_____

Mark the end date on your weekly schedule. On that date, make an appointment with yourself to come back to this page and write the results you have noticed.

_____

_____

_____

Sheila

Sheila flopped down on the couch, crushing her math assignment as she landed. "I can't understand it," she wailed. "I studied three whole hours last night for that algebra test. How could I get a *B* minus?" She kicked off her shoes with such thrust that they bounced off the wall. The cat leapt up and fled to the kitchen. Sheila flipped on the TV. A *Buffy the Vampire Slayer* rerun. Good, she thought. At least I'll have some company while I read the next chapter. I've just got to do better on the next exam! How can I win a scholarship with a *B* minus in algebra?

Sheila leaned back, tucked her feet up under her, and snuggled into the cushions. She pulled the coffee table closer so that she could reach the potato chips. She opened her algebra book and started on chapter 3. It was all about quadratic equations. A potato chip crumb bounced off her chin and landed somewhere on her new T-shirt. "Drat it!" she said, jumping up to brush off the chip. That's when she noticed that Buffy had come face to face with the real Dracula. "Oh, I remember this one," she said, as she sat down again, this time with the bowl of chips in her lap to watch how Buffy handled this formidable foe.

Just then Amy came knocking at the screen door. "Come on in," said Sheila. "I'm just working on my algebra. Hey, did you see they're doing an article on most eligible homecoming dates in the school paper? I bet they'll include that new guy, Fred what's his name…."

The hour slipped by almost unnoticed.

"…so anyway, I guess I better keep working on algebra. I'm determined to pull up this grade. Say, Amy, you do well in math. What's your secret?"

"Nothing special," said Amy, thoughtfully. "Well, I do try to set up my room so that I can really concentrate. And I review and practice my math in small pieces, every day. That's how I study my Spanish, too. It works real well for me. My math teacher says studying math is like studying a language. You know, each piece builds on the one that went before. It's really hard to catch up if you get behind in math."

"Thanks, Amy," said Sheila, bounding up from the couch. "You've given me an idea. And now I've got some work to do."

Fast-forward to a week later and see Sheila at work on her algebra. She's sitting at the kitchen table after dinner. The table is clear except for a basket of pencils and paper that she brought from her room, her algebra textbook, and

(continues)

(continued)

her notebook. She has told everyone "no visitors or phone calls while I'm in my algebra zone." The kitchen is tidy and quiet. Sheila's only companions are the cat curled up at her feet and the steady sloshing of the dishwasher. She's been studying her algebra at this time and place every day for a week and is beginning to like it just fine. She can concentrate here, and algebra is starting to make some sense.

The adult Sheila laughs when she thinks back on those nightly sessions in the kitchen with the cat and the dishwasher. When she has a thorny problem to work out at the physics lab, she still puts herself mentally back in her study zone, where her brain had its first real chance to tackle math.

Quiz

1. Your conscious mind processes _____, then _____ it in your memory warehouse and _____ it when you need it.

2. Information enters your brain through the senses of _____, _____, _____, _____, and _____.

3. How can you help your brain take in a big, ugly, confusing topic?

   _____

   _____

4. The little elves in your memory warehouse need plenty of _____ and plenty of _____ to help you sort out concepts.

5. To remember a fact you have just learned, what should you do?

   _____

   _____

6. Name five things you *need* in your study zone. _____

   _____

   _____

_____

_____

_____

7. Name six things you *don't need* in your study zone. _____

_____

_____

_____

_____

8. When studying, take a two-minute stretch break every _____ minutes and a walk-around break every _____ minutes.

9. New habits take about _____ days to get established.

10. Develop good study habits to _____ poor study habits.

True or False?

11. You should study at different times and in different places because your brain works better with a little variety. T F

12. Study your hardest subject last. T F

13. Your brain works better if you do all your reading assignments together in one long session. T F

14. Finding links between your study topics and your own life makes learning more effective. T F

CHAPTER 3

Listening and Taking Notes in Class

The classroom is a very special place. It's like a stage for an important event: the transfer of knowledge from the teacher to the students. Each person there has a role to play. The teacher is cast as "the expert," the source of wisdom and knowledge. The student plays the role of "the novice," eager to learn the answers to all of life's questions.

Maybe it doesn't play quite like that in your classes. But there are certain roles and expectations for teachers and students. The education system has written scripts for both of you. But each person brings unique talents to the action. The transfer of knowledge is acted out over a number of episodes, often with a rather entertaining cast of characters.

This chapter is about skills you can develop to help you learn better in the classroom. It's also about how to play your student role to the hilt. With a little effort, you can rewrite your script and even win rave reviews.

Be a Class Act

A principal player in the classroom is your teacher—a human being with strengths and weaknesses like everyone else. What does this mean to you?

- **Teachers tend to judge students by how they act—it's human nature.** Think about this when you choose how to act in class.

- **Like other human beings, teachers want to be liked.** They basically try to do a good job, and they respond well to signs of interest. Teaching and grading papers is hard work, and your interest and involvement in class might be your teacher's most valuable reward.

- **Turn in assignments that are neat, orderly, and clearly legible.** This is especially important in math class, where daily handwritten homework assignments may make up a large portion of your grade.

- **When you treat the teacher with courtesy, you create a "halo effect."** Your teacher will view you in a positive light, which will shine on all your class work.

The teacher, although human, is playing the very serious role of educator. You can be totally charming in class, but your teacher still expects you to play your part: Teacher teaches—student listens, studies, and learns. The teacher can't learn it for you.

In fact, teachers would probably much rather just engage you in a Vulcan mind meld to transfer their knowledge. Because that's not possible, they present their knowledge in small steps, in the order they think you will learn it best. They also try to start interesting discussions. They know this draws you out and helps you connect new ideas to what you already know.

Teachers' educations outfit them with a good set of tools to help you learn, including lectures, visual aids, exercises, and hands-on experiences. The teacher can adapt these tools to fit your particular strengths and weaknesses.

Teachers really do want you to learn and do well on tests, so they give lots of hints, suggestions, and direct instructions about what and how to study. If you open your mind to these clues, you've learned an important secret to getting better grades. But to do this you have to listen and look—and think—in class, as you'll see in the next section.

In fact, your best role as a student is to make the teacher's role as easy and enjoyable as possible—if you want to earn better grades, that is. Get with the program. Show interest in what the teacher is trying to do. Participate in the transfer of knowledge. If you're not a model student now, that doesn't mean you can't audition for a better part.

Consider these tips:

- Maybe you've been asking questions that reveal that you have not read the material, not listened in class, and not paid attention to instructions. Start asking questions that show you have thought about the material.

- Maybe you never say a word in class. Perhaps it's because you're shy or lack self-confidence. Try preparing for class discussion with a few points that you understand and can talk about.

- Maybe you give up when you've read the textbook and listened in class, but still don't understand something. Try talking to the teacher after class. Chances are, the teacher will respond to your desire to learn and will steer you in the right direction.

- Maybe you're afraid you ask dumb questions. Good teachers will say, "There's no such thing as a dumb question." What they mean is that they want to help you understand. Your question tells them whether they are succeeding. Ask questions that show you are trying and thinking. Your teacher will appreciate your interest, and that translates into better grades.

A final note about teachers: As human beings, they have different strengths, just as you do. Some give interesting lectures, some are good at encouraging students, some have a knack for citing good examples, and some can spark good class discussions. Some you'll admire, and others you'll barely tolerate. Just remember, it's not all up to the teacher. Your role as student is to play an active part in the transfer of knowledge. It's up to you, too.

 ## Driven by Distractions?

Think about the subject in which you've chosen to improve your grades. Close your eyes and picture yourself sitting in that classroom with your fellow students. The teacher is explaining the subject and writing on the chalkboard.

Now conjure up all the details of the room and the people: sights, sounds, smells, the feel of the desk, and so on. When you have a clear picture in your mind, notice all the things other than the teacher that attract your attention. List them here:

_____

_____

_____

(continues)

? Driven by Distractions? (continued)

_____

_____

How do you think you could make these things less distracting? Write down at least two ways:

_____

_____

_____

_____

_____

Develop Good Listening Habits

How good a listener are you? Do the teacher's words seem to go in one ear and out the other? Are you tuned in to what your fellow students are doing in class instead of the material you need to know for the next test?

If your listening is less than perfect, you're not alone. Research shows that people miss about 75 percent of what they hear. Listening is not that easy, and here's why: Your mind thinks a whole lot faster than people speak.

"Wait a minute!" you're saying. "If thinking is so much faster than speaking, why do I miss so much of what I hear? Shouldn't there be plenty of time to catch up to what the speaker is saying?"

The problem is that, while the teacher speaks, your mind is racing way beyond the subject. It's easy prey for the other sights and sounds of the classroom. Let's face it, your conscious mind—no matter how eager it is to tune in—faces stiff competition from all that goes on in class.

The good news is that you can develop better listening habits. You can train your mind to stay focused by following a few simple guidelines. These help you work with your brain, not against it.

Prepare to Listen

1. **Prepare for class.** You've no doubt heard this before: Do your home-work. It's important. Do all your assigned reading and work the prob-lems. You'll come into the classroom more confident and ready to participate. Your teacher plans the class work based on the assumption that you've completed the outside assignment. That assignment is like a framework on which you can hang new pieces of information. If you do the reading and the problems, listening is much easier. You have an idea of where you're going. You give your brain a fighting chance to be interested in what the teacher has to say.

2. **Bring the tools you need.** These could be pens or pencils, notebook, textbook, eraser, compass, ruler, calculator…whatever the class requires. You need these tools to keep good records of class work. Your goal is to be well prepared when you enter the classroom. You can't afford to waste time sharpening pencils or looking for your ruler while the teacher is talking. Get in the habit of doing a mental checklist of tools you'll need before you head for class.

3. **Arrive a few minutes early.** Are you in the habit of dashing into class at the very last minute? If so, this simple tip will go far to improve your focus. Arrive early enough to find a seat, shuffle your papers, stretch, or daydream before class begins. You'll have a clearer mind to focus on listening and taking notes.

4. **Sit up front.** If you're free to choose your own seat in the classroom, sit as close to the teacher as possible. Your goal is to position yourself where you can see and hear everything the teacher presents. This is the mate-rial you need to learn to be a top student. Four additional reasons to sit close to the action: You capture more of the details. You're less apt to be distracted by noisy, giggly, fidgeting, belching, note-passing classmates. Your teacher will see you and remember you as actively involved. (This helps when the teacher must decide between a *B+* and an *A-*.) You'll be less tempted to take a nap or stare out the window.

5. **Review your notes.** Take just a minute or two to glance over your notes from the last class session. This refreshes your memory for where you left off, and readies your mind for further input.

Actively Listen

6. **Listen with your whole body.** When class begins, sit up straight, lean forward, hang on every word. Get your whole body involved. This will help you stay alert.

7. **Listen with your whole mind.** This is not the time to do homework for the next class. Give yourself completely to this class. Your mind will wander every so often, and that's natural. When it does, just guide it gently back to the subject. Use the time while the speaker pauses to ask yourself questions about what you just heard or to summarize the ideas in your own words.

Keep a Record

8. **Take notes.** This is the most powerful way to improve your listening and get better grades. Notes are a brief written record of what you see, hear, and do in a class. In the next section, we'll show you step by step how to take good notes.

Remember, you're in charge, so use these tips to get everything you can out of your class time. No matter how boring the subject is, good listening habits can actually make it more interesting. Even the most boring teachers seem to blossom when they feel students are paying attention.

A+   Mini-Quiz

What are the eight steps to better listening?

1. _____

2. _____

3. _____

4. _____

5. _____

6. _____

7. _____

8. _____

Take Good Notes

Quite simply, taking notes is your ticket to good grades. The reason is simple: Almost everything you need to learn to make top grades is presented or referred to by your teacher during class—lecture details, comments about homework, descriptions of class assignments, and so on. And some topics the teacher talks about in class aren't even in your textbook, so you can't always expect to fall back on the book if you haven't taken notes.

Listening draws only on your sense of hearing. Taking notes brings your other senses into the action. It turns the spoken word into written words that you can visualize. The act of writing involves your sense of touch and movement. You're helping to feed your brain the rich diet of pictures, sounds, and touch that it needs. As a result, you remember much more of what you hear. Plus you can refer to notes again and again. That's much easier than trying to remember what the teacher said in a lecture.

As a bonus, the details you capture on paper serve as a study checklist. Good notes tell you exactly what to study to do well on a test.

The following sections tell you how to master the mechanics of note taking and capture the essence of what the teacher is saying.

Master the Mechanics

Here are seven steps to taking more powerful notes:

1. **Organize your notes.** Teachers try to present topics in an order that you can understand—starting with the simple topics and moving to the complex ones. So it makes sense to keep your notes in the same order. When it's time to prepare for a test, you'll have a book of notes presented in logical order. Get a separate notebook for each course or a binder with a tab for each course. Start each day's notes on a new page and put your name, the date, and the main topic of that class at the top of the page. Whatever you do, don't tear out your note pages, fold them up, and stick them inside your textbook! It's too easy to lose them that way.

2. **Leave "thinking space."** Don't fill up the whole page with writing. Leave about one-third of the page blank on the left side. Record your class notes in the two-thirds at the right. Later you can use that empty left column to record key words, names, dates, formulas, diagrams, and other things you want to remember. The left column is then like a checklist of things to study for your tests.

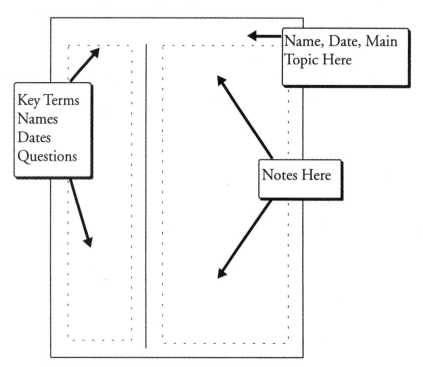

3. **Use the note-taking style that works for you.** People write notes in lots of ways, depending on their own preferences and the subject matter. Notes don't have to be just words. You can draw pictures, highlight with color, or make charts and lists. Use your own personal note-taking style—any method that shows the words have passed through your brain on the way to your notebook page. You'll find three examples of note-taking styles later in this chapter.

4. **Use your own brand of shorthand.** Can you write as fast as your teacher can talk? Probably not, but you can keep up with the key points if you use your own short forms of words. For example, suppose your instructor says:

"I want you to remember that a small pencil is more valuable than a large memory."

You might pick out the key words and jot down the following:

     ✓ *sml pencil more val lrg memory*

The check mark at the left stands for "I want you to remember" or "This is important"—a clue that this might show up on your next test.

An important hint: Be sure not to abbreviate key terms or unfamiliar words until you have spelled them out at least once in your notes for that day.

5. **Right after class, reread your notes.** Fill in any missing words and letters that you need to make the meaning clear. Do this while the class is fresh in your mind. Within 10 minutes after class is best, but within 24 hours is the next best. If you wait much longer, a lot of dust will have settled on those ideas and you may not be able to understand your own shorthand.

6. **Write legibly.** Your notes won't always be neat, but they must be readable. Write so that you can read and understand what you've written. You don't need to spend valuable time rewriting your notes later, unless you find that this helps you better understand the material.

7. **Save the teacher's printed notes.** Your teacher may hand out information sheets in class. Some handouts tell you about homework assignments. Others tell you about tests or list key words, names, and formulas you need to remember. Add these to your notebook near your handwritten notes on the same subject. You can bet these will be questions on your next test.

Taking Notes in Outline Format

Outlining is the most rigid note-taking method, with a set structure of letters, numbers, and indentations. Taking notes in outline style forces you to organize the material as you go. If the teacher's lectures are easy to follow, this method is the best way to keep up your concentration.

Here is an example of class notes taken in outline format. Notice how each topic has subtopics under it. These subordinate topics are indented more than the main topic. The system also alternates between using numerals and letters to number each topic. The most important topics are noted with Roman numerals. Topics under those are noted with capital letters. Topics under those topics use Arabic numerals. And topics under those topics use lowercase letters.

I. Civil Rights Movement 1954-1960

    A. Blacks turned to courts to end school segregation

        1. Bec. Congress wouldn't act—too controversial

        2. 1896 Plessy vs. Ferguson upheld "separate but equal"

        3. 1954 Brown vs. Bd. of Education of Topeka changed all that

            a. "separate ed. facilities inherently unequal"

            b. argued by Chief Just. Earl Warren

        4. 1955 Brown II ordered states to integrate schools "w/all deliberate speed" (i.e., go fast slowly)

    B. Resistance to integration

        1. Pres. Eisenhower didn't push it

            a. "laws couldn't change what's in people's hearts"

            b. afraid to anger south. politicians (Dixiecrats)

            c. but had to uphold fed. law (e.g., in Little Rock)

        2. "Southern White Citizens" formed to work against Brown vs. Bd. of Ed.

    C. 1957 Little Rock, AK, school desegregation—key event!

        1. Nine blacks tried to attend all-white Central High School

        2. Gov. Orval Faubus ordered 270 national guardsman to keep them out

        3. Eisenhower sent fed. troops to enforce Brown vs. Bd. of Ed. and maintain order

Freeform Notes

When a lecture is difficult to organize as you listen, you can simply record short paragraphs using key phrases. Leave a line of space when the teacher seems to be moving to a new topic. Indent phrases that provide details or examples. When you review your notes later, you can underline the main points to better structure the material for study.

Civil Rights Movement 1954-1960

Congress wouldn't act to end school segregation—too controversial—so <u>blacks turned to courts</u>

    1896 Plessy vs. Ferguson had upheld "separate but equal"

    In <u>1954 Brown vs. Bd. of Education</u> of Topeka, Chief Just. Earl Warren argued "separate ed. facilities are inherently unequal"

    Supreme <u>court ordered states to integrate</u> schools "w/all deliberate speed" (i.e., go fast slowly), 1955 Brown II

    Pres. <u>Eisenhower didn't push it</u>—"laws couldn't change what's in people's hearts"; afraid to anger southern politicians (Dixiecrats)—but had to uphold fed. law (e.g., in Little Rock)

    <u>Group formed to work against</u> Brown vs. Bd. of Ed., called Southern White Citizens

Key event: <u>Little Rock, Ak, school desegregation 1955</u>—nine blacks tried to attend all-white Central High School

    Gov. Orval Faubus ordered 270 <u>national guardsman</u> to keep them out; when Eisenhower had him remove the guard, hostile mobs of whites surrounded school

<u>Eisenhower sent fed. troops</u> to enforce Brown vs. Bd. of Ed. and maintain order

Mini-Quiz

What are the seven steps to taking more powerful notes?

1. _____
2. _____
3. _____
4. _____
5. _____
6. _____
7. _____

Mind Mapping

Mind mapping is a technique that can help you capture the structure of a topic by using key phrases and positioning to show relationships. It's especially useful for summarizing notes that you made using the outline or free-form styles.

Start with the main concept in the center of your notebook page. Then add key points as spokes of a wheel. Supporting details extend on lines from each key point.

You can add points at any spot in any order. Plus, you can draw arrows connecting similar thoughts at different spots in your diagram.

Mind mapping has many uses besides taking notes. Try it when you're studying for tests or organizing a term paper topic. (We'll cover tests in chapter 7 and term papers in chapter 5.)

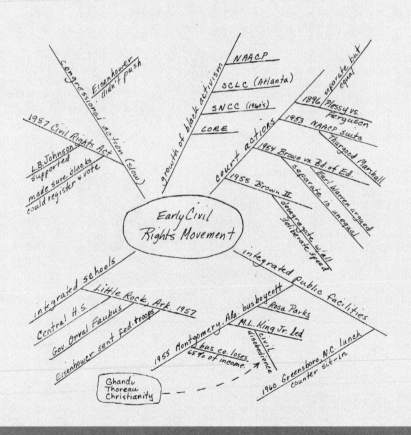

Note-Taking Shorthand

Here are some suggested symbols and abbreviations you can use to take notes faster. You can probably add to this list with lots of symbols and abbreviations of your own. Just be sure you know what they stand for!

Abbreviations and Symbols	
&	and
@	at
bec	because
b/4	before
→	causes, produces
←	caused by
=	definition
esp.	especially
etc.	etcetera, and so on
e.g.	for example
>	greater than, more than, larger
i.e.	in other words
<	less than, smaller, fewer than
#	number
¶	paragraph
p	page
pp	pages
+	plus
re	regarding, about
§	section
∴	therefore
thru	through
×	times
w/	with
w/i	within
w/o	without

(continues)

Note-Taking Shorthand (continued)

Notations to Yourself

★	to do
✓	study this information for a test
?	missing information
??	didn't understand

Choose Your Methods and Use Them

Which of these tips do you think will most help you improve your grade in your chosen subject? Write which ones you plan to follow:

_____

_____

_____

_____

_____

Set a goal to use your chosen tips for two straight weeks in that class. What do you expect will be the result?

_____

_____

_____

Capture the Essence

"Sure," you say, "I can master the mechanics of note taking. But how do I really know what to write and what not to write?"

You could just try to write down everything the teacher says, exactly as it comes out of the teacher's mouth, like a tape recording. But like a tape recording, your notes would show no sign that they ever passed through your brain.

Good notes hit the highlights of class, and that takes some brainwork. Your aim is to record the main ideas that the teacher talks about, along with supporting details. You also want to include key terms, phrases, and questions that help jog your memory.

Taking notes in math class is more difficult than in other classes because you want to write every step of the problems, and that makes it difficult to listen to the explanations. In fact, sometimes there isn't time to stop and think. First and foremost, you have to make sure you record everything on the blackboard.

To know what to write, you need to know what to look and listen for. Here are some tips.

What to Listen For

- **Word clues.** The teacher uses words to highlight what is important for you to know. For example:

  "The most important reason..."

  "The event had three causes..." (listen for the *three*)

  "This will be on the test..."

- **Voice emphasis, body language.** The teacher changes the pitch of his or her voice, or pauses, or uses gestures as natural ways of emphasizing important points.

- **Repetition.** Saying the same thing different ways is designed to help you learn a concept. Especially tune in when the teacher repeats the same sentence using the same words. This is a strong hint that you should write it down exactly as the teacher has spoken it and then memorize it.

- **What the teacher says during the first and last minutes of class.** Introductions and summaries often preview and review the main ideas the teacher is trying to get across. These moments are prime time for listening and taking good notes.

- **Ideas that relate to a previous lecture.** Write these down because they help build links that organize what you know, making the new material easier to remember.

- **Ideas that relate to the textbook readings.** Draw these connections to deepen your understanding of the material.

- **Ideas that relate to your personal life.** These ideas are especially valuable because they suggest realistic examples for you to think about.

- **Good questions from students.** If a question brings out good discussion, it may show up as an essay question on a test.

- **Possible test questions.** If you pay attention, you can spot material the teacher will ask you about on a test. You'll get better at this as you become more familiar with your teacher. For example, as the class ends, your teacher says "Oh, by the way, read page 52 of your textbook before we meet again." Write this down in your notebook and place a check mark next to it. The check marks will signal material that's likely to appear on your next test. Don't be surprised if you're quizzed on the material on page 52 the next time your class meets.

- **Instructions for how to do homework, what to study for the test, and so on.** Teachers are amazed at how often students ignore direct instructions. If you write them down—and follow them—you'll get better grades.

What to Look For

- **Anything the teacher writes or circles on the chalkboard.** This is the teacher's way of emphasizing the material. Be sure to copy it carefully.

- **Diagrams, charts, or lists that the teacher draws or points out.** These are excellent visual organizers for material that would be hard to explain using words alone. Copy them into your notes.

- **The teacher's original class goals for the topic you're studying.** Your teacher may have distributed a listing of the topics that would be covered in class this semester and listed the learning goals for each. Refer to this handout and verify that you have a grasp of these topics. Also, your state or local school corporation may publish its system-wide goals for this subject, so it helps to be familiar with these goals as well.

When you see or hear these cues, write down as much information as you can capture. Each idea that your teacher presents could reveal the answer to a test question. As a general guideline, try to write between one-fifth and one-third of what you hear. Take notes on what you don't know rather than on what you already know. But in math class, you should record 100 percent of what you see, and only then add explanatory notes alongside examples and solutions as time permits.

If the teacher talks too fast for you to keep up, write as much as you can, and add a big question mark in your notes. This is a signal for you to go back and ask a question, look up the subject in another textbook, or discuss the missed material with a friend. Keep checking or asking until you understand everything you're required to learn and record it in your notebook.

In math class you may find it difficult to record problems from the blackboard as well as the explanations of the steps of the solution the teacher gives. In this case, try to get all the information from the board first. Later you can go over your notes to see whether you understand each step. If you don't understand the steps to the solution, you can ask the teacher to go over it again with you.

Use these techniques to capture the essence of each class period. The active listening you use to draw out the highlights brings about the transfer of knowledge better than anything else. Later, studying the highlights will help you organize the supporting details that you wrote down. When the highlights show up as test questions, you'll be prepared to earn better grades.

A⁺ _____
Mini-Quiz

Name five clues you should listen and look for in class that will tell you what you need to know.

_____

_____

_____

_____

_____

Note-Taking Exercises

1. Try out your personal shorthand by recording the main ideas from a TV documentary or the evening news. Then "report" the main ideas to family or friends.

2. Draw a "mind map" of this chapter, capturing the main ideas and supporting details.

Attend Every Class

The only way to be sure your notes are complete is to attend every class from start to finish. You can spot likely test questions just by coming to class and listening. You also need to hear important announcements regarding schedules and test times that the teacher makes at the beginning and end of class. Absence and tardiness do more to destroy your effectiveness than lack of out-of-class study time.

The first day of class is especially important. At the first session, teachers often reveal exactly what you need to do to get top grades in that class. You may receive a course outline, long-term assignments, test schedules, learning goals, and so on. The teacher may also talk about how you'll be tested and the factors that will determine your final grade.

If an emergency arises and you must miss a class, talk with your teacher. Find out what was covered while you were gone (but don't expect the teacher to repeat the whole lecture for you). Ask whether the teacher gave out any printed notes. It is also possible that the homework assignment will be posted on the teacher's Web site, so be sure to check it. See whether one or two of your bright classmates will share their notes with you. Their notes are a poor substitute for being in class yourself, but they'll help you catch up.

There's another good reason for perfect attendance: Each class lays the groundwork for further learning. This is especially true of foreign languages and mathematics. The teacher presents topics step by step in logical order. Being there now will help you understand topics presented in future sessions.

If you miss a class, you have to play catch-up. If you miss two or more classes, you fall behind in your work and may never recover. You can easily avoid this hardship: Attend all of your classes. Learning is a whole lot easier one step at a time.

Milton

Milton lived to play football. He had trained hard and had won a top spot on the school team. He was the envy of his friends and the pride of his coaches. But Milton wanted more. He knew that good colleges were looking for good scholars, not just athletes. He knew he needed to do something about that *B–* in history.

Milton took a hard look at his listening habits in history class. Most days he would arrive barely in time for class, slip into the back row, slouch down in the chair, and keep one eye on the teacher while he drifted into daydreams … leaping in slow motion to snatch a forward pass … shedding the grasping linebackers … sprinting across the goal line … beginning his famous victory dance, warmed by the glow of adoring fans….

Milton realized he had to change his ways. He decided to start some new habits: to come to class early, to sit near the front, to concentrate on taking good notes, and to review his notes before and after each class. He set a goal of following these habits for two full weeks, until the next test.

(continues)

(continued)

On Monday morning the teacher was surprised to see Milton at the front of the class. She was pleased to see that he seemed to be paying attention. She knew he was a star football player, but Milton had never stood out as an especially good student in her class.

As the week wore on, Milton stuck to his goal of starting new classroom habits. He felt more prepared for class and even took part in discussions. His mind still wandered out on the playing field now and then, but he practiced guiding it gently back to the classroom. He concentrated on picking out the highlights of the teacher's lecture. He wrote down as many details as he could. This helped to keep his mind on history. In fact, he really got interested in the Civil War when the class discussed how John Brown led the uprising at Harper's Ferry.

At the end of two weeks, Milton reviewed his history notes carefully to prepare for the test on Monday. He walked into the test feeling prepared. And what a nice surprise! Almost every question was about something he had written in his notes. When test grades were handed out, the teacher said, "Nice work, Milton." He looked at his test paper and smiled. He had aced the test.

Quiz

1. The classroom is a stage for the _____ of knowledge.

2. What role are you expected to play in the classroom? _____

   _____

   _____

3. Cite at least three ways that teachers are like other human beings.

   _____

   _____

   _____

4. What is the "halo effect"? _____

   _____

   _____

5. Why do teachers give hints, suggestions, and direct instructions about what and how to study? _____

_____

_____

6. Explain the difference between good and bad questions students ask in the classroom. _____

_____

_____

7. Describe two techniques you can use to keep your mind focused while the teacher is pausing or writing on the board. _____

_____

_____

8. The most powerful way to improve your listening is to take

_____.

9. Why should you leave "thinking space" in your notes? _____

_____

10. Describe the three styles of note-taking illustrated in this chapter. How do they differ? _____

_____

_____

11. To help yourself remember what you heard in class, _____ your notes within 24 hours.

12. What should you do with printed handouts that the teacher gives you in class? _____

_____

13. What clues can you listen and look for to be sure you catch the main ideas and facts that the teacher is trying to present? _____

_____

_____

True or False?

14. Speaking is faster than thinking. T F

15. Listening to the teacher is more interesting if you prepare for class. T F

16. It's best to arrive in class at the last minute to keep your mind sharp. T F

17. Listening is easier if you have a framework on which to hang new pieces of information. T F

18. Most teachers are happy to repeat a lecture for you if you miss class. T F

19. Attending the first day of class is important. T F

20. Borrowing good notes from a bright classmate is just as good as attending class yourself. T F

21. When taking notes in math class, be sure to record notes and explanations as you copy problems from the board. T F

CHAPTER 4

Read with a Purpose

The higher your grade level in school, the more reading you're asked to do. By the time you reach college, reading will be a major part of your studies. You won't be going to school for the rest of your life, but you will be reading. Whether you use reading skills on the job, for learning how to repair the faucet, or just for fun, you'll need good reading skills.

Undoubtedly, there are some types of reading that you love to do—maybe novels, fan and fashion magazines, or comic books. Wouldn't it be great if you could devour all your school reading in the same way? If you set a purpose, preview your reading, read actively, and review faithfully, you'll be surprised how much more rewarding your school reading can be.

The tools in this chapter can help you read more effectively to improve your grades now. They'll also set you up to enjoy reading for the rest of your life.

Evaluate the Reason for Your Reading

Reading isn't just reading to take in words, sentences, and paragraphs. It's reading for a reason. The writer had a reason for writing the words, sentences, and paragraphs. You have a reason for reading them. Your reason has everything to do with how you should approach the reading task.

Here are examples of some different kinds of reading you probably do, with reasons you might have for doing each. Can you think of specific materials you have read that match each type of reading in the table?

Type of Reading	Purpose
Pleasure	To relax, to transport your mind to a fantasy world, to enjoy the stimulation of other people's ideas
Previewing	To prepare for a class, to decide whether a book contains the type of information you need for a research project
Skimming	To get the overall idea, to locate specific facts you are looking for
Careful reading	To remember the main ideas and related details, to figure out how you agree or disagree with the author
Intensive reading	To be able to re-create what you read, for example, to follow step-by-step instructions for hooking up a stereo system

Each type of reading demands a different approach. Each requires a different level of concentration. As you read about the techniques in this chapter, think about which ones you could apply to each type of reading you do.

 ## What Do You Love to Read?

Maybe it's not your textbook, but a magazine, the latest book from your favorite novelist, letters from friends, "how to" books, and so on. Your leisure-time reading can tell you something about how you can read your textbook well. Think about how you feel when you read your favorite material. Why do you read it? What are you looking for? Do you remember what you read? What makes you remember it? Write the answers here in a short paragraph.

_____

_____

_____

_____

_____

_____

Enter Your Reading Zone

Some types of reading really put your brain to the test. So think about how you can work with your brain, not against it, when you do assigned reading. All the suggestions in chapter 2 for setting up a study zone apply to getting your mind ready to focus on reading, too. You need good light, a comfortable temperature, few distractions, and a place to sit up straight (not in bed!) and concentrate. To position the book for low glare and easy viewing, prop it up at a 45-degree angle.

Give yourself time to settle into a good concentration mode. Then take stretch breaks every 15 minutes and walk-around breaks at least every 50 minutes.

An ideal place to do reading assignments is the library. It's tidy, quiet, and well lighted, and has plenty of straight-backed chairs. When you really need to read intensively, find a cubbyhole away from the main aisle. Train yourself not to look up every time someone walks by.

Preview the Text Before You Read It

Don't launch into reading until you know where you're going. Reading is much easier and faster if you first map out the territory. The way to do this is called *previewing*.

Begin each reading session with a preview of coming attractions. It's like stretching and warming up before heading to the starting line of a race. It gets your mind in gear, gives you a reason to read, and suggests the best approach to take.

Your preview may take 2 minutes or 15 minutes, depending on the type of reading you are doing. You might worry that previewing just slows you down. But give it a try. You'll find that this small time investment pays big dividends when you get down to the business of reading.

Here are three steps to effective previewing:

1. Establish the purpose of the reading.
2. Look for the structure.
3. Form questions about the material and guess the answers.

The following sections explore some of the details of these three steps.

Establish the Purpose of the Reading

Ask yourself why you are reading this material. Is it for fun, to see a different viewpoint, to stimulate your ideas, to fill a gap in your knowledge, or to decide whether it contains information for your research paper? Are you reading to memorize something in detail for a test, to get an overview of a subject, or to teach yourself step by step how to do something?

If you don't hold the answer yourself, look for clues from the teacher and the author. Consult your class notes to see whether the teacher mentioned why this reading was important and how it would apply to your class work. Read the preface to learn why the author wrote the book.

Whatever the purpose of the reading, match it up to your own personal reason: to get a better grade, to understand the world better, to have more interesting things to talk about with friends, or whatever.

Look for the Structure

The person who wrote what you are reading took great pains to organize the subject matter in step-by-step fashion so that you could understand it. The writer probably formed a picture of you in his or her mind and asked: How can I convey what I know and love about this subject to my reader? How can I build up a mental picture in the reader's mind to help my reader learn and remember the material?

The writer divided up the topic into chapters, topics, subtopics, lists, and other logical chunks that you could understand. The main ideas and supporting details were then written within that logical structure.

The more you grasp the structure that the writer set up, the better mental map you will have for organizing your own recollection of what you read.

The overall structure makes the details make more sense, and you will remember them more easily.

A Structure-Identification Exercise

Most books have a lot of clues to help you recognize the structure and purpose of the material. Pick up any textbook and find each item in this list. Then pick up any library book and do the same. What kinds of information does each item give you about the subject matter?

Item	Textbook	Library Book
Front and back cover, dust jacket		
Table of contents		
Preface		
Introduction		
Index		
Chapter introductions		
Chapter learning objectives		
Topic headings (in larger, heavier type)		
Subtopic headings (smaller than topic headings)		
Topic sentence (usually the first or second) of each paragraph		
Words made to stand out by underlining, italics, or bold type		

(continues)

(continued)

Item	Textbook	Library Book
Numbered and bulleted lists		
Tables, charts, diagrams		
Illustrations with explanations		
Special features (boxed or otherwise highlighted to stand out from the main text)		
Chapter summaries		
End-of-chapter questions, exercises		

Form Questions, Guess the Answers

As you scan the chapter titles, topic headings, and key words, turn each one into a question. This energizes your mind to lock onto specific issues and grasp any details that might answer the questions. Ask yourself *who, what, when, where, why,* and *how.* Make the questions lively and interesting. Here are a couple of examples:

> "What would I have done if I had been president then?"

> "What's it like to be a teenager in Zaire?"

Then guess what the answers might be. Draw upon what you already know about the subject. You'll make important links to your storehouse of knowledge. You may find you already have a partial framework for learning the new material. Then the material won't seem so unfamiliar.

Reading Time

Time yourself reading a textbook for four minutes. Then divide the number of pages that you read by 4. This is your average rate per page for that particular subject. Use this rate to plan how much time you need to complete your daily reading assignments in that class. On your weekly schedule (see chapter 1), allow ample blocks of time for these assignments. Include extra time before and after your reading blocks to preview and review the text.

A⁺ Mini-Quiz

What are the three steps to effective previewing?

_____

_____

_____

Read Actively

After you finish previewing the text, you're ready to read quickly through the material. Just engage your mind, and off you go.

If you're doing careful reading, as in studying a textbook chapter, read each paragraph quickly for the main idea. Then pick out one or two supporting details and any key terms.

If you own the book, highlight or underline the main ideas and details. But don't highlight everything in sight, or else you'll lose the power of this active reading technique. Highlight just the top 10 percent of the material. *Hint:* Don't highlight anything until you've read the entire paragraph. You can't be sure which is the main idea until you've followed the writer's complete thought. If you don't own the book, jot down in your notebook the key words and phrases as you would record a class lecture. Label them as notes from your reading.

Get more than just your eyes involved in reading. Involve your whole body, mind, and imagination. Draw a picture of what you're learning. If you're reading literature or a play, try to "hear" the voices of the characters. Read key passages out loud to hear what they sound like. "Feel" yourself into the picture.

If you're reading about the circulatory system, you can "be" an oxygen-hungry red blood cell, carried on a swift current through the bloodstream. Hear the loud *ka-thunk, ka-thunk* as you approach the heart. Feel yourself being swooshed through the heart and lungs and catapulted back out into the aorta. Sounds crazy, right? But surely you've seen *Inner Space* on TV or ridden *Body Wars* at Disney World? It's the same idea, and there's no better way to "get into" the topic you're reading about than to imagine yourself in the middle of it.

Feed your brain a rich diet of pictures, sound, and touch that packs all the ideas from your assigned reading neatly into your memory bank.

Every now and then, however, your mind is bound to wander. It's the same old problem of the mind moving faster than the eye and letting itself be open to any distraction. Just corral your mind gently back to the task at hand. Remind it how happy you'll be when your good reading habits net you a better grade.

Reading Mathematics Assignments

Reading mathematics is different from reading other subjects. For example, if you're working on a report for history or literature, you might be expected to read 40 pages in one evening. A reading assignment in mathematics, however, is typically only two or three pages per evening. Unfortunately, most students skip the reading and proceed directly to the homework problems. Most students then return to the reading assignment only to consult the examples and look for clues to help them complete their homework. The disadvantage of this approach is that when students encounter problems that differ from the examples, they are stuck. Rather, you should prepare for a reading assignment in math as you would any other reading assignment and add a few other helpful items as well.

Every time you sit down to read mathematics, have paper and a pencil handy. You'll need to write things down as you go along. You'll also need them to work through the examples step by step. Other items you might need include a calculator, a protractor, and graph paper. Chances are good that you'll need these items to look at some calculations, copy a diagram, or graph some equations.

One important thing to keep in mind: Don't rush! A good reader of mathematics may linger over the meaning of a couple of sentences for several minutes. This is your opportunity to think about concepts that might have been mentioned in class, but you were too busy copying down everything on the blackboard to absorb it all.

Finally, it's more than likely that there will be a few practice problems at the end of the reading. Don't skip these. Work through the practice problems and make sure you understand them before tackling your homework assignment.

Speed Reading: Is It for You?

There's a way to read much faster than you are used to. It's called *speed reading*. The idea is to train your eye to see line by line, not word by word. Line-by-line reading helps your reading rate catch up to your brain's fast pace. There's less time for your attention to wander, so you absorb more of the material.

When you read a line of text, your eye does not scan smoothly from one end of the line to the other. It jumps from point to point, focusing each time it lands.

When you first learned to read, your eye probably jumped from letter to letter until you sounded out a whole word. As your skill improved, your eye jumped from word to word. Chances are, your eye now jumps to four or five spots per line, taking in two or more words at each focal point.

All speed reading does is train you to take in larger groups of words at a single focus—maybe two to three jumps per line. If you get really good at it, you can take in a whole line of text at one focus. You might then run your finger right down the center of the page to pace your line-by-line reading.

To get a feel for speed reading, try reading the following words of storyteller Nathaniel Hawthorne. Do not read individual phrases word by word. Instead, follow the dots in a straight line from the top of the page to the bottom. Let your eye pause briefly at each dot. See whether you can take in the phrase below it at each pause.

•

The moonlight glistened

•

on their steely scales,

•

and on their golden wings,

•

which drooped idly over the sand.

•

Their brazen claws,

•

horrible to look at,

•

were thrust out, and clutched

•

the wave-beaten fragments of rock,

•

while the sleeping Gorgons dreamed

•

of tearing some poor

•

mortal all to pieces.

•

The snakes that served them

•

instead of hair seemed

•

likewise to be asleep;

•

although, now and then

•

one would writhe,

•

and lift its head, and thrust out

•

its forked tongue, emitting a drowsy hiss,

•

and then let itself subside

•

among its sister snakes.

Try this several times. How quickly can your eyes move from dot to dot? Do you still grasp the meaning?

Some people think speed reading makes you lose the meaning of the text. But research shows that speed readers actually understand better what they read, because their minds have less chance to wander. Speed reading works especially well if you combine it with the other techniques described in this chapter.

You can take classes or buy material that will help train you in speed reading. Ask your reading teacher for recommendations, or visit Web sites such as the following:

Speedread America   www.speedread.org

Speed Reading 4 Kids   www.speedreading4kids.com

RocketReader   www.speedreading.com

A⁺

Mini-Quiz

How is reading math assignments different than reading English assignments?

_____

_____

_____

What is the purpose of speed-reading?

_____

_____

_____

Review for Recall

You've come to the end of the text. Now what? Put the book away and go have some fun? Not just yet. Invest just a few more minutes in refreshing the mental pathways to the new ideas you have just learned.

Ask yourself the questions you made up during your preview. Try answering them out loud, in complete sentences. Ask yourself how you could use this information in your daily life.

Look back over the highlights of the text you read. Get a feel for the order and structure of the subject matter. Write a summary in your notebook, using your own words. Make lists out of things that seem to go together.

Your review may reveal areas that you still don't understand. Mark each of these with a big question mark. Make a point of following up until you get them straight. Often a different viewpoint helps. Try reading about the same topic in a different textbook or on a Web site. The other author may do a better job of explaining the parts you didn't understand. Or, look it up in an encyclopedia, talk it out with a friend, or ask the teacher to go over it in class. Don't give up until you understand it.

Review time after reading is an important secret for improving your grades. Give yourself this short time to ponder the text before getting back to your daily routine. You'll thank yourself for this little gift when you discover how much easier it will be to study for the next test.

A⁺ Mini-Quiz

What are some tips for reviewing what you've read?

_____

_____

_____

_____

Think About Improving Your Reading Skills

Think about the subject in which you have chosen to get a better grade. How important are good reading habits to your mastery of that subject? Explain.

_____

_____

_____

This chapter suggested many ways to improve your reading habits. Write which suggestions you plan to use in your chosen class. Set a goal for how long you plan to try them out.

_____

_____

_____

_____

_____

_____

Greg

Reading was the last thing Greg ever had on his mind. He wanted to be doing, not sitting. He wanted to be with people, not cramped in a chair with his nose in a book. He wanted to make things happen, get people organized, accomplish things. How better to prepare himself to wheel and deal in the business world, a dream he had held ever since he earned his first five dollars mowing a lawn.

Now in his junior year, Greg was beginning to think seriously about colleges. He wanted to do everything right, so he sat down with his guidance counselor to make a plan. "You know, Greg," said the counselor, "you could stand to pull up these grades in English and history. This is a critical year for establishing a good grade-point average."

"It's reading," said Greg. "I get so bored with it, it takes me forever, and I just can't sit still that long." "But Greg," said the counselor, "maybe you don't realize how much reading you'll have to do in your college courses. And someday when you're a CEO, you'll spend a great deal of time reading reports from the field. Maybe you need to work on your reading skills."

Greg thought about this during the next few days. He really wanted to pursue his dream, but his dream was closely tied to reading, which he hated. He thought about the tradeoffs he would have to make—taking some time away from his leadership projects to work on reading skills now, earning better grades, and getting into a good college. Doing all these things would give him a chance to read effectively in college, earn better grades, and get into a better business school. It seemed like a good deal. "I'll make it happen," said Greg out loud.

From a book, Greg learned some tips for improving his reading skills. He set up a timetable to try out the techniques. As he worked "previewing" into his routine, it somehow felt familiar.

That Saturday, the cross-country team, of which he was captain, was running at a school across town. During the half-hour before the race, the coach jogged the team slowly along the cross-country course, over the hills and through the woods, past the shed, and around the football field. As they jogged, the coach pointed out course markers and terrain where they would have to run cautiously because of mud and tree roots. As the start of the race neared, the team warmed up by touching their toes and leaning into trees to stretch their calves and ankles. That's when a light went on in Greg's head.

"Hey, this warm-up is just like previewing when I read! I get a picture of where I'm going, and when I start reading, I'm ready to read without stumbling and hesitating. Good deal!"

At the starting gun, Greg leaped out ahead of the huge pack of runners, inspired by his recent insight. "Whoa, slow down; you gotta pace yourself," he remembered. He did pace himself and finished with a personal best time.

As the months sped by, Greg practiced his new reading techniques with his textbooks and his English literature. He previewed, highlighted, took notes, wrote summaries, and took a few minutes after each session to think about how the reading might apply to his own life.

The nicest thing Greg discovered was that, when he read with a purpose, reading went much faster. He actually finished his assignments sooner than he used to. He liked this, because it gave him more time to be with friends and perfect those "people" skills that someday would help him run ahead of the pack in the business world.

Quiz

1. Describe five different purposes for reading. How would your course and speed differ with each type of reading? _____

   _____

   _____

   _____

   _____

   _____

2. How can you work with your brain, not against it, in doing your reading assignments? _____

   _____

   _____

3. While previewing your reading, establish the _____, look for the _____, form _____, and guess the _____.

4. When your mind wanders during reading, what can you remind it of to keep it focused? _____

_____

5. Every time you sit down to read mathematics, have _____ and _____ handy.

6. The principle behind "speed reading" is to read _____ by _____ instead of word by word.

7. If you do not understand the material in a reading assignment, what four sources can you look to for help? _____

_____

_____

_____

_____

True or False?

8. Previewing your reading saves time in the long run. T F

9. When you read your textbook, underline or highlight at least 50 percent of the material. T F

CHAPTER 5

Writing Papers and Presenting Oral Reports

Do you spend the school year lurching from one crisis to another? Are you dealing with just what's due today and unable to think several weeks ahead? Then this chapter might help you lead a calmer life. You'll feel a greater sense of control and reap more rewards—such as better grades. The secret lies in good planning. Good planning enhances all kinds of school-work. This chapter focuses on planning (and completing) two kinds of long-term assignments that you're sure to face: writing a paper and presenting an oral report.

Plan for Excellence

Why do teachers assign projects, papers, and oral reports? They want you to learn something, and it's not just the subject matter. They want you to learn how to think ahead and organize your work to complete long-term projects on time. The skills involved in planning and organizing will come in handy in the future, both in your personal life and in your job. They're worth every moment of the time it takes to learn them now.

The goal of project planning is to spread the work out over time so that you have a fighting chance to do a good job. The result of good planning is a predictable series of steps which, if you follow them as planned, complete your work on time—with no time crunches, no last-minute crises, and no headaches. Project planning is a powerful tool for working smarter rather than harder. It makes schoolwork easier and less of a hassle.

? Perfect or Panic?

When was the last time you completed a long-term assignment outside of class? Was it a paper? A science project? An oral report? Thinking about that time, what was the hardest part? How did you feel while you worked on it? How did you feel when the work was done? What result did you get? What would help you do an even better job next time? Write a brief paragraph summarizing that experience here.

_____

_____

_____

_____

_____

_____

_____

_____

Here's an eight-step program for planning your next project:

1. As soon as you hear about your long-term assignment, schedule a block of "planning time" within a day or two. At the appointed hour, go to your study zone with a clean sheet of paper and all your notes about the assignment.

2. At the top of the paper—your "planning sheet"—write the name of the assignment (for example, *English term paper*) and the due date. Also mark the due date on your calendar or weekly schedule (see chapter 1 for more on weekly schedules). Take note of how many days away that date is and what other activities you might have planned between now and then.

3. Read through your notes about the assignment with these questions in mind:

- What is the teacher asking you to do?

- What is the project's purpose?

- What exactly are you expected to turn in (for example, a 10-page paper plus a bibliography, a 5-minute speech with visual aids, a science display with a 3-page summary of your research, or a PowerPoint presentation)?

- Are there printed instructions? Any special requirements for how the end product should look? Any particular format it should follow?

Spend enough time with your notes to fully understand the assignment. Then summarize the assignment in your own words at the top of your planning sheet.

4. Now sit back, relax, and turn on your mental projector. You're going to watch a "movie" of yourself doing that project. Watch yourself getting started, perhaps picking a topic first. See yourself heading for the library and the Internet to gather research materials. See yourself reading and taking notes…making an outline or sketching ideas on paper… interviewing people…doing your experiment…zeroing in on what you plan to say. Keep the film rolling while you sit down to write…revise… type…proofread…or build…or draw. Enjoy the happy ending when you show up in class, rested and confident, to turn in the assignment.

As movie director, you want to include all the details that make the story come to life. Think of everything that you might need to complete your assignment: activities, materials, equipment, people, costs, even some elbow grease.

5. When the movie is over, sit back up and write down what you saw. What were the main stages of the project (for example, topic selection, research, first draft, revisions)? Which activities made up each stage? Get every step of the process on paper.

6. Now put the steps in order. For each step, think of everything you need to do in order to get ready for the next step. Number the main stages *1, 2, 3,* and so on. Then number the activities within the stages *1A, 1B, 1C…2A, 2B,* and so on.

7. From your mental "movie" you probably gained a sense of the time that each step will take. Estimate how many hours you need to complete each step. Write the number of hours next to each step. Total up the hours.

8. Now make a plan. Look at your due date. How many hours or days do you have to work between now and then? Set your deadline for project completion a few days before the real due date. You need this "fudge factor" to allow for events beyond your control. Then set a deadline for each stage of the project. Look at the following sample planning sheet to see how to set up your own.

Sample Planning Sheet

American History Term Paper

Today: October 15

Due: December 3

Time Available: Approx. 6 weeks

Assignment: Write research paper on the spirit of reform in pre-Civil War America. Pick one example of reform movements (utopianism, prison reform, labor reform, temperance, educational reform, etc.) and describe it in detail. Relate it to growth of industry in U.S. Length 10 pages, plus bibliography (see written instructions!).

Steps:

Startup (1 week)

    Read for overview of reform movements

    Select topic (example of reform mov't)

    Write rough outline

Research (2 weeks)

    Gather materials from library

    Look up articles and sites on the Internet

    Read and take notes

    Write detailed outline

Writing (1 week)
    First draft (reserve time on computer!)
    Footnotes and bibliography
Final Prep. (1 week)
    Review and revisions
    Grammar and spelling check
    Final typing (reserve computer)
    Proofreading and corrections
Start Date: October 16   My Deadline: November 27

You'll be tempted to set your start date for several days or weeks from now, but don't. Set it sooner, not later.

More than anything else, planning puts time on your side—time to ponder, time to come up with good ideas, time to make good ideas even better, and time to revise and polish. Give yourself this time by planning wisely. You'll do yourself a great favor!

Come to Terms with Term Papers

Everything we said about assignments applies double to writing a term paper. Research papers take time. Give yourself as much time as possible. Here are some how-to tips to take the bite out of long-term writing projects.

Pick a Do-able Topic

There's an art to picking term paper topics. Consider these points:

- Avoid a topic so huge that whole libraries have been published about it (for example, "World War II").

- Steer clear of a topic so narrow or unusual that you'll find scarcely any research materials (such as "The Role of Army Dentists in the Normandy Invasion").

- Find the happy medium (like "The Impact of the Normandy Invasion on the Course of World War II").

If possible, pick your topic from a subject area that interests you; you'll approach the research and writing with more enthusiasm. The topic should require a reasonable amount of research. It should also lend itself to making and supporting several main points. Some teachers will ask you to call your paper's main theme a *thesis,* and then your paper's purpose will be to prove (or disprove) your thesis.

Pay close attention to the required length of the paper. That should tell you how large a topic you can dig into. When you have a topic idea, get your teacher's opinion. He or she will help shape your idea into a topic you can handle.

Evaluate Source Materials

When you have an idea of the general subject area you'd like to write about, head for the library. Look up the subject in the online catalog. Browse through the book titles to get a feel for the number of books the library has on this subject. To find articles about the subject in recent magazines, look up the subject in the *Reader's Guide to Periodical Literature.*

To find articles on the subject on the Internet, go to a search engine (such as Yahoo!, Google, Lycos, Excite, AltaVista, and so on) and type the subject in the Search box. Just be careful to evaluate the results and use information only from reliable sources. Just because it's on the Internet doesn't mean it's true. (See the appendix at the end of this book for a listing of Web sites that can help you get your research started.) You can also search online bookseller sites such as Amazon.com and find the very latest books on the subject. If your local public library doesn't have that book, they can try to get it for you on interlibrary loan.

Pick out suitable books and articles and preview them using the techniques described in chapter 4. You'll quickly learn whether they're right for your research. Previewing techniques also let you know how manageable your topic is.

While you're at the library, don't overlook the encyclopedia. For a quick introduction to a subject, look it up in a children's encyclopedia. That simple overview can help you keep your bearings as you read more details in other books and articles.

Prepare Source Cards

When you find the books and Web sites that will be most helpful to your research, get yourself a stack of 3 × 5 cards. On separate cards, write all the publication facts about each book or article, which you will need to prepare the bibliography. For Web sites, you can print the page, highlight the information you want, cut it out and tape it to a card, and write the Web site name on the card. (You could also use computer files to organize your sources and notes, but they aren't as portable as the good old note cards your grandparents used when they wrote their term papers for school. So why mess with a good thing?) Do this now, at the beginning of the project. Save yourself the headache of scrambling to retrieve those books and Web sites when you're typing the final pages.

For each book or article, make up a unique code to identify it. This can be a number, the author's last name, or a shortened title, as long as you use the same coding system for all the sources. Write the code on the card. Use this same code on notes that you make from this source, so that you can properly credit the material later in footnotes.

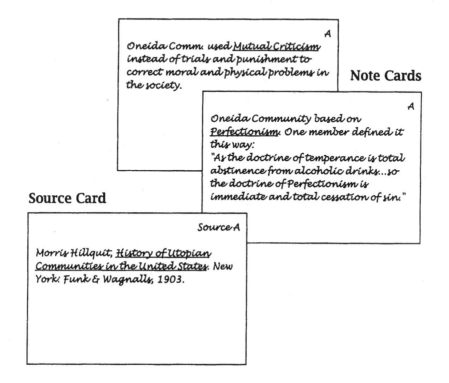

A

Oneida Comm. used *Mutual Criticism* instead of trials and punishment to correct moral and physical problems in the society.

Note Cards

A

Oneida Community based on *Perfectionism*. One member defined it this way:
"As the doctrine of temperance is total abstinence from alcoholic drinks...so the doctrine of Perfectionism is immediate and total cessation of sin."

Source Card

Source A

Morris Hillquit, *History of Utopian Communities in the United States*. New York: Funk & Wagnalls, 1903.

Draft the Basic Structure

Now that you've surveyed the source materials, you should have a better idea of the direction you want to take with your topic. Make a rough outline or mind map of your paper now, before you begin carefully reading the source materials. This will help your mind latch onto any facts that relate to your paper topic. List the main points you intend to make, and fill in any supporting details that you already know. A mind map is especially useful at this stage. It lets you sketch out your ideas in whatever order they come. You can impose a definite order later, after you read the source materials.

Just Do It!

Are you completely overwhelmed by the thought of a class project? Don't know where to begin? Don't paralyze yourself with thoughts of gloom and doom. Use the eight-step planning program from earlier in this chapter. Then pick any 5- or 10-minute task from your planning list and just do it! Starting with a small, manageable task will unlock your paralysis, get your momentum going, and make you feel competent rather than helpless.

Research and Record

Now you're ready to dig into your topic. Read your source materials carefully, looking for details to support the points you want to make. Make notes on things you don't already know. Many students use 3 × 5 or 4 × 6 index cards for this purpose. Write only one complete thought per card, and be sure to include the source code. Write the thought in your own words. This helps you think about what it means. If the source says it so well that you want to quote the original, put quotes around the material so that you can tell it apart from the thoughts written in your own words. Be sure to give proper credit to the source in your paper; otherwise, you will be caught for *plagiarism* (stealing an author's words and using them as your own) and will probably get an automatic failing grade on your paper.

Draft a Detailed Outline

After you have read the source materials, it's time to nail down the specifics of your paper. Deal out your stack of note cards. Put them in piles that relate to the points you sketched out in your basic structure. If any don't fit those points, see whether they suggest an additional point you could make. You may want to completely regroup the cards in another structure that makes more sense. You may also want to discard a few cards that don't relate clearly to the topic.

Now develop a detailed outline or mind map for your paper. This should combine what you have written on the note cards with what you already know. You're not just rehashing what you found in your source books. You're interpreting what you learned. You're applying your own structure.

In your outline, spell out the major sections of the paper. Then develop the topic sentences around which you will build paragraphs. Include phrases to remind you of the supporting details. Your organization may shift around a bit as you write, but this outline serves as a detailed map to guide your way.

Use your outline to help you plan your writing time. Schedule blocks of time for different sections, with breaks in between. If you spread the writing over several days, set mini-deadlines for different sections.

Now, Write!

If you use the system described so far, writing the first draft of your paper should be easier than you imagined. You can make it even easier by following these tips:

1. **Sleep on it.** The evening before you start writing, review all your notes and your outline. While you sleep, your brain will start organizing for the next day's writing task.

2. **Get in the mood.** When it's time to write, go to your study zone (or, if you're writing your paper on your computer, go to the place where the computer is). Give yourself 10 to 15 minutes to sharpen your pencils, shuffle your papers, and ease your mind into a ready state.

3. **Start anywhere.** The hardest thing to face is the blank page or the blank computer screen. Sometimes the good opening paragraph doesn't come easily. Begin with whichever point most interests or inspires you. Once you're on a roll, you can go back and write the beginning. Using a word processing program makes it even easier to rearrange your paragraphs after you write them.

4. **Talk to a friend.** Right in the middle of writing? Well, yes, in a manner of speaking. Write as if you were telling what you've learned to a friend—a friend eager to learn what you know. Write in your own "voice" using your own words, as you would write to a friend. Aim for clear, simple language. Don't load it down with million-dollar words and fluff.

5. **Don't demand perfection yet.** You can tie yourself up in knots if you try to compose perfect sentences on the first draft. Aim to get all your ideas on paper rather quickly and in a logical order. By all means, write in complete sentences. But count on at least one round of revisions to approach your idea of perfection.

Read for Meaning

You've been a movie director and then a writer—now be Michelangelo. Think of your rough draft as a big block of marble. You're going to hammer and chisel it into a work of art.

Read through your draft with a critical eye. Does every paragraph make a point? Does that point relate to your paper topic? Can you move paragraphs around to develop your ideas more clearly? Could you choose more precise words? Can you smooth the transitions from section to section? Pay special attention to your first and last paragraphs. They should introduce and summarize your paper topic in your very best prose.

Read for Style

Just when you thought you were done, you need to read through your paper once more—out loud. This time it's a check for grammar, spelling, and punctuation. Read it out loud to find the rough edges that you need to polish. If something sounds awkward, try rephrasing it. Check the spelling of any odd-looking words. If you're writing on a computer, take advantage of the spell-checking and grammar-checking features.

Also be sure that your report, especially all its notes and references to your sources, follows a set format. Your teacher will show you where to find examples of the format he or she wants you to use.

Prepare the Final Version

You've come up with good ideas, written them clearly, and polished them to a fine sheen. Now you need to present them for approval.

Don't skimp on this important step. You need to

- Present a neat appearance.

- Follow the teacher's instructions on format, bibliography style, and so on.

Use the best method you have available to produce the final draft—neat handwriting, typing, or computer printout. Your paper doesn't have to be fancy, just tidy, readable, and error free. With proper presentation, your work of art will stand out in all its glory—and earn a better grade!

Conquer Oral Reports and Speeches

How do you feel about speaking in front of the class? Do your knees tremble? Do your palms sweat? Does your voice crack? You're not alone. Public speaking is on almost everybody's top 10 list of most feared things to do. In fact, we often hear that many people would rather die than speak in public! Luckily, making a plan, and sticking to it, overcomes much of the fear.

The same steps you should follow for term papers—planning, selecting a topic, researching, outlining, writing, and reviewing for meaning—apply to preparing an oral report too. The difference lies in the presentation: During an oral report, you stand face to face with your audience. The following sections present some secrets to help you prepare.

Connect with the Audience

Think about how you can push the right buttons in your listeners so that they sit up and take notice of what you have to say. Plan an opening statement that gets their attention. If you can do that, they'll be with you all the way, and your job will be easier. For example, begin with an intriguing question or something funny. Your listeners will relax and enjoy the show.

You should give special emphasis to transitions between sections of your talk so that you can keep your audience with you. Signal the transition by asking a good question or repeating a new idea in different words.

Give some thought to a snappy ending, too. Listeners need to know when you're done. If you end with a flourish, you might get a round of applause. People just naturally respond that way to good endings. And if the teacher senses that the class enjoyed your presentation, he or she might be more inclined to give you a better grade.

Show and Tell

Visual aids can help you present your ideas with ease. Pictures, hands-on demonstrations, charts, summaries of main points, and multimedia presentations all help bring home your points. They're also very useful for organizing your talk. A set of visuals gives you props to talk from. You can ask a transition question to fill the gap while you grab for the next visual. Try taping a 3 × 5 card to the back of each visual aid, with your notes for the speech. What could be easier? You might also enhance your presentation with audio and visuals produced on your computer, such as a PowerPoint slide show or some accompanying music or sound effects you have put on a CD.

Leave Time for Practice

Don't compose your speech at the last minute. And don't wait till the curtain rises to see what you're going to say! You need time to craft your talk and to practice it.

The first few times you give a talk, write out exactly what you plan to say. Then read it out loud several times. Soon key phrases will cue entire sentences. Jot these key phrases on 3 × 5 cards, or sketch them on a mind map.

Include phrases that help you make smooth transitions and a good ending. Then practice delivering the speech using just these notes. The more you practice, the more confident you will be when you face the audience.

Stand and Deliver

If you put time on your side, practice good planning, and follow your plan, you'll have no more sweaty palms, knocking knees, and stomach butterflies! But you'll still feel keyed up. That's natural, and it will actually help you be "on" for your presentation. But you won't be tempted to run and hide under the nearest desk.

If possible, do a quick run-through a few minutes before you are scheduled to speak. Read through your written speech to bring all the details back to the front of your mind. Then take a few deep, relaxing breaths, stride up to the front with confidence, and go for it!

The good news is, the more you talk in front of an audience, the more comfortable you'll feel. Give yourself every opportunity. When you taste the special feeling of having the audience with you, you may get hooked on public speaking. That's good, because it's a life skill you'll use again and again.

Use These Suggestions for Your Own Project

Do you have a class that requires a long-term project such as a term paper or oral report? Could that project benefit from the suggestions in this chapter? Write which techniques you plan to use and what results you expect.

_____

_____

_____

_____

_____

Juanita

Juanita felt a wave of nausea as she heard the teacher assign a five-minute "speech to convince" for a week from Friday. Juanita had a strong mind and a great awareness of other people, but that very combination made her painfully shy. All her life, she had managed to avoid speaking in public. She died a thousand deaths just thinking about getting up in front of a group. What would she find to say? How would she hide her embarrassment? Maybe that Friday she'd just call in sick.

Juanita was scared silly, but she had a tough streak. She knew she wanted to make a mark on the world, and her shyness might always hold her back. It was time to face the music. So Juanita laid out a schedule for choosing a theme, finding data to support her points, outlining her thoughts, and writing a draft. She would complete the draft by Wednesday, leaving a full three days to practice.

As she finished each task in her plan, Juanita felt a little less scared. She picked an interesting topic, and enjoyed reading about it in the library. She began to outline her main points, and remembered she needed to connect with the audience.... The audience!!! That old fear welled up and Juanita broke out in a cold sweat. But wait a minute. Who was that audience? Just her school friends, after all, thought Juanita. She imagined her classmates growing fangs and horns, sprouting wings and long tails, drooling, hissing, and belching great flames. She exploded into giggles at the thought. This image helped her relax, and she decided to make a joke about it at the beginning of her speech.

By Wednesday morning, she had the makings of a good speech. A good beginning, pretty good transitions, a poster to talk from, and a definite ending. Wednesday afternoon, she read the draft through three or four times, fine-tuning the words to make them more natural. Then she underlined the key phrases and drew a mind map to help her remember them. She taped this to the back of the poster.

As Friday approached, Juanita felt reasonably confident, but now and then little flames of dread still licked at the corners of her brain. She still couldn't picture herself actually getting up there and delivering the speech. But she stuck to the plan.

Juanita practiced giving the speech out loud from her notes. She practiced over and over, and pretty soon a picture began to form in her mind. It was her, in class, preparing to give her speech. She saw herself stepping up to the front...introducing her topic (the audience laughing at her joke!)...moving smoothly through the main points...showing details from her poster...and closing with a clear, firm voice.

And that's exactly how it happened Friday morning. There was no applause after that first speech, but Juanita felt proud that she had stood up to her fear and helped herself by using good preparation. And there was plenty of applause—in fact everyone stomped and cheered—when Juanita ran for student government the next year and made a rousing appeal for improvements in school safety.

Quiz

1. Rearrange these project-planning steps into the proper order. Put a number next to each one to show where it goes in the process:

    ____ Make a plan with deadlines for each step.

    ____ Estimate hours for each project step.

    ____ Schedule planning time.

    ____ Write down the main steps of the project.

    ____ Watch a "movie" of yourself doing the project.

    ____ Read project instructions carefully.

    ____ Put the project steps in order.

    ____ Make up a planning sheet.

2. On the subject of picking a term paper topic, Goldilocks would probably advise "Not too _____, not too _____, but just _____."

3. Before digging into your research and taking notes, it's wise to write a rough _____ of your paper.

4. The point of dealing out your note cards in stacks is to clarify the _____ of your paper.

5. List five ways to overcome "writer's block" when writing your first draft.

6. Describe the steps that turn a rough draft into a polished term paper.

7. To present an interesting oral report, you need to connect with the
   _____.

8. In delivering speeches, pay special attention to beginnings, endings, and
   _____.

9. You can complete long-term assignments with fewer hassles if you
   _____ them before you begin.

True or False?

10. It's good practice to write a paper that's shorter than the required length, so your teacher can spend less time reading it. T F

11. A children's encyclopedia might be useful in researching your paper topic. T F

12. Previewing techniques are not useful when doing library research. T F

13. You should prepare source cards after drafting your paper. T F

14. Most people enjoy public speaking. T F

CHAPTER 6

Review and Memorize What You've Learned

In this book, you have read about several methods to engage your mind in listening and reading, rather than just go through the motions. Thoughtful reading and listening are your best preparation for the day when your teacher wants to see how well you've learned the material. But even if you've followed those methods, you need a refresher to get ready for a test.

Do you recall the image of your memory as a huge warehouse from chapter 2? The doors are guarded by the five senses—hearing, sight, touch, smell, and taste—which like a rich and varied diet. The conscious mind works on storing ideas and facts in logical places. We talked about how important it is to review a new fact (as in your class notes) soon after hearing it for the first time, to establish a good trail to its location. The more often you call up the fact, the better your conscious mind knows where to find it.

In this chapter we present study techniques to make sure your conscious mind can retrieve all those ideas and facts when you really need them—at testing time.

?

I'd Like You to Meet...

Have you been introduced to someone new lately? What do you remember about that person? The color of his shirt? His name? His brand of shoes? The sound of his voice? His scent? The texture of his hair? How that person treated you? Which people you were with at the time? The location of your meeting?

How will you "know" that person the next time you meet? Write your answer here:

_____

_____

_____

Notice the way you remember a new person. It's a clue to how you can study more effectively for tests.

Review What You've Learned and Make it Your Own

During the days before a scheduled test, begin reviewing your class notes and reading highlights on a regular basis—every day if possible. You should also look over your worksheets and graded homework. This repetition lays down pathways for retrieving information. It also gives the little elves in your memory warehouse some time to rearrange concepts for better understanding. If it's a math class in which you're trying to improve your grade, keep up with the homework and do extra review practice to keep yourself sharp.

As you review, follow these tips to start you down the path to easy recall.

Organize It

First you need to organize in your mind all the information that has been presented to you. Make sure you identify and understand the main ideas that you will be tested on. Understand the other concepts that support the main ideas. Determine how the bigger and smaller ideas relate to one another. By doing this, you will develop a framework on which to hang new information as you learn it.

Sense It

Use all your senses to develop a vivid picture of each idea or procedure in your mind. Sensory images are the language of the subconscious mind. You dream and think in living pictures that include sounds, sights, and the sense of motion and touch.

Remember the new person you were recently introduced to? The things you noticed during that encounter point to the senses you should be sure to involve in studying:

- If details of the person's appearance stick with you, use pictures to help yourself study.

- If you were struck by the person's voice, recite facts to yourself out loud to involve your auditory ability.

- If you noticed textures of clothing and hair, or focused on the layout of the room where you met the person, "feel" yourself into a scene where you can touch the idea or position yourself near it in space.

- If you noticed the people around you and how they treated you, maybe practice quizzes with a friend would help you remember.

Connect It

Associate each idea to others that you are studying and to facts you already know. Is this idea like or different from this other idea? Which ideas go together? What does this set of ideas lead to? What happens because of this idea? Build up a structure of ideas in your mind.

Absorb It

Soak up an idea like a sponge. Read about the idea in your notes. Then review the description in the textbook. Then read about it in an encyclopedia. Then ask a trusted friend to describe it to you. If you see and hear the idea in all of these different forms, it becomes like a part of you.

See It, Say It

This is a useful technique for memorizing key terms, historic dates, definitions, foreign-language words, theorems, and formulas one at a time. Read your notes about one item, and then cover the notes and repeat what you read out loud. Review and recite. This is the principle behind flash cards. In fact, you could make your own set of flash cards to help you study for your next test. You might use them to help you remember the meaning of vocabulary words for French class, or for formulas and theorems for math class. Put the question on one side and the answer on the other. Use them to quiz yourself, or have someone else quiz you with them.

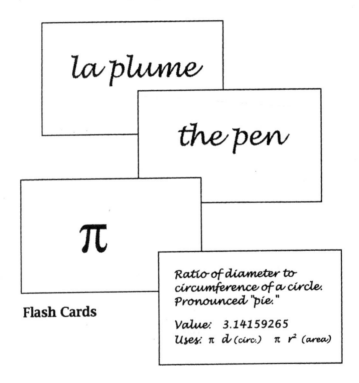

Flash Cards

For learning math, it is often very helpful if you can explain a procedure to a classmate or be able to write it down in your own words.

Practice It

If you are studying mathematics or sciences, practice applying formulas in a variety of problems and settings. Even if you don't grasp the idea behind the formula at first, you may be surprised to find that repeated practice actually leads to better understanding. If you are studying a foreign language, practice using vocabulary words in a variety of sentences.

Live It

Some school subjects seem very far away from your own experience. You can make them more real if you imagine yourself looking at the subject from inside rather than from the outside. "See" the Civil War from the viewpoint of a Georgia plantation owner or a Gettysburg schoolteacher. To understand the complex food chain of the rain forest, "be" a creature who lives there.

Ask It

Guess what the teacher will ask you about each fact or idea. Then state how you will respond. Review earlier tests to see the types of questions the teacher asked.

Keep at It

Repeat all these techniques until the material sinks in. When you know it, you'll know it.

Refresh It

If you follow these methods, you'll do well on your next test. But if you want to retain material over a longer period of time, you need to review it regularly. Quickly read through all your notes once a week, and thank yourself when you find how easily you study for your final exam.

Buying Time

Long line at the movies? Boring bus ride? Pacing in the laundry room while your jeans finish drying? These little 10-minute waits are ideal times to bring out your notes or flash cards and do some quickie memorizing. Turn throw-away minutes into quality (and painless) study time. These little pieces of time add up to better grades!

Mini-Quiz

A⁺

Name the ten tips for pre-test reviewing.

_____

_____

_____

_____

_____

_____

_____

_____

_____

_____

Use Super Memory Tricks to Recall Details for Tests

Sometimes just recalling main ideas and relationships is not enough. You need to nail down the supporting details as well. Names, faces, dates, formulas, terms, spellings, and lists—you may need to recall these, without fail, for a test. Or you may need to remember an important phone number or address for personal reasons. Super memory tricks—also known as *mnemonics* (ni·mon´·iks)—could be the answer.

Right now, do you see a pink elephant in front of you? Think about how your brain processes that question. Your conscious mind rummages about in your memory warehouse. It retrieves a mental image of an elephant and applies the color pink. Then it compares that mental creation to what you see in front of you right now. It does not find a match, so you answer "No, I don't see a pink elephant." As you can see, your brain is very good at making mental pictures and linking one mental picture with another.

You can use that talent to help you remember things. For example, suppose tomorrow is trash pickup day. You have a busy day planned, and you want to be sure you remember to take out the garbage can to the curb. So you place a wastebasket right in front of your door. When you head for the door tomorrow morning, you see the wastebasket in this unusual place. That triggers a mental picture of you putting out the trash.

The following memory tricks help you commit just about anything to memory. They're all based on your brain's natural ability to link one thought with another. The trick in each case is to form an unusual, exaggerated link that really sticks in your memory.

Brain Cartoons

Mental pictures that are concrete, fanciful, silly, larger-than-life, and full of sound and action are powerful memory aids. Here are some examples showing how brain cartoons work:

- You're memorizing vocabulary words for an SAT test. The next word is *jovial,* defined as "full of playful good humor." Your task is to form a brain cartoon that links the word itself with its meaning.

  First, look closely at the word, *jovial.* You slice it in two parts: *jo vial.* You picture a 50-foot giant named *Joe.* He's playing with a 10-foot tall *vial.*

  Now, add the meaning. The vial is full of laughing gas. Joe is doing party tricks with the vial, tossing it into the air and balancing it on his chin. He is full of *playful good humor.*

- Now you're proofing your term paper, and you're not sure whether you spelled *believe* correctly. It seems you've had to look up this word in the dictionary many times. Maybe a brain cartoon could help you remember it correctly.

  You divide the word into three pieces, *be li eve* (pronouncing it "bee" "lie" "eve"). You see a wacky 20-pound **bee** that's grown a long nose, like Pinocchio, because it told a **lie.** You see it buzzing about at your window in the **evening,** with the moon and stars as background.

These are only examples of the picture-links that are possible. Brain cartoons are your very personal creations. Make them as vivid and striking as possible —the odder the better.

Stroll Down Memory Lane

Pick a place that you know well, like your house or apartment building. Mentally walk through that place, noticing things like entrances, hallways, and rooms. Think of the route that you would follow to walk through the entire building. Now you have a wonderful way to remember things in order—like the main points of your speech, or the steps of an experiment. Think of each as something you'd encounter along a route.

Let's say you've used this technique to learn the first 10 presidents of the United States in order. Your mental walk-through might go something like this:

1. You approach the house from the sidewalk. A huge dollar bill is pasted across the front door, with the picture of George Washington in full view. *(Washington)*

2. You open that door and enter the front hall. There you are greeted by a naked Adam—with modesty fig leaf, of course—handing you an apple with a big bite out of it. *(Adams)*

3. Take a left turn into the living room, where a young son wearing a big *J* on his T-shirt is romping over the couch and easy chairs. *(Jefferson)*

4. Stroll into the dining room, where a very angry young boy is stomping his foot and refusing to eat his spinach. *(Madison)*

5. Next stop is the kitchen, where you find a gorgeous blonde cooling herself in front of the open refrigerator. *(Monroe)*

6. In the back hall, there's that Adam handing you an apple again, but this time he's wearing a hot-pink sweatshirt adorned with the letters "J.Q." *(John Quincy Adams)*

If you have a long list to memorize, add your favorite path through the neighborhood and notice all the sights you would encounter on your walk—the old oak tree, the corner road sign, the haunted house, and so on. Using moving images of your house, school building, or neighborhood and your own creative pictures, you'll think of memorable ways to recall all kinds of things in order.

Eight on the Garden Gate

Another handy way to remember a list is to use number-picture associations as "pegs" on which to hang the list items. This is a three-step process.

First, pick out a word that rhymes with each number, for example:

one—bun

two—shoe

three—tree

four—door

five—hive

six—sticks

seven—heaven

eight—gate

nine—mine

ten—pen

Next, create a vivid mental picture of each word. For example, for *eight,* see a white picket fence with a gate swinging open and creaking noisily in the wind. For nine, see a dark mine shaft with the blackened face of a coal miner, digging away.

Once you make these mental links between pictures and sound-alike numbers, you have a ready-made memory aid to use in many situations. The remaining step is to add visual images to the links you have already formed.

Try it out in biology class to remember the seven systems of the human body:

1. **Alimentary:** See a huge gurgling stomach lying on a hot dog *bun* and slathering itself with mustard.

2. **Respiratory:** See pale gray lungs stuffed in a giant *shoe* and breathing in and out.

3. **Nervous:** See a trembling person sitting high on a *tree* limb, visibly worried about falling.

4. **Integumentary:** See a *door* made out of living human skin, with downy hairs and freckles.

5. **Musculoskeletal:** See a dancing skeleton, wearing a buzzing bee *hive* for a hat.

6. **Reproductive:** See a heap of *sticks* and hear strange crying sounds from deep within; carefully lift the sticks one by one and find a litter of baby kittens sheltered underneath.

7. **Endocrine:** See fat little glands, decked out with banners like "adrenal" and "thyroid," arriving at *heaven's* pearly gates, and St. Peter turning them away because their hormones have been acting up.

Creative Acronyms and Sentences

Make words out of the first letters of a set of facts you need to memorize. What are the names of the Great Lakes? No problem. Visualize HOMES on a lake, and you'll remember Huron, Ontario, Michigan, Erie, and Superior. Remember "Every Good Boy Does Fine"? Your music teacher will be pleased that you can recall the notes that go on the lines in the treble clef: EGBDF.

You can use the same idea to remember key words. Take the first letter of each one and make up a weird sentence that sticks in your mind. For example, to recall the names of the seven systems of the body, make up a sentence using the letters *A, R, N, I, M, R,* and *E.* It might be something like "Artistic rodents needle ice monsters riding eagles." Then devise a zany brain cartoon to capture this odd scene.

Rhyming Verses

"In fourteen hundred and ninety-two, Columbus sailed the ocean blue" has worked for many a grade-schooler who wanted to remember when Columbus discovered America. If you're a closet poet, rhyming verses may be your best memory aid. Try capturing the three states of matter in poetic meter:

> There once was a free little **gas**
> That frolicked in air, but alas!
> It caught cold and condensed
> To a **liquid** and thence
> To a **solid** and quite frozen mass.

Just pick out what you want to memorize and make a verse out of it. You'll be surprised how easily you'll remember it.

Rhythm and Beat

You can often memorize numbers and formulas by reciting them out loud to your own creative rhythm and beat. That's probably how you learned your phone number.

You might try this in chemistry class when you need to memorize Avogadro's number, 6.02×10^{23}, which is the number of molecules in a mole of gas. Like a cheerleader, shout "six point oh two, times ten to the twenty-third!" Shout it again and again until you develop a beat. Pretty soon you'll be hearing it in your sleep. Surely you'll remember it for the chemistry test.

Number Games

Sometimes you can remember a large number by playing a game with it. A large quantity such as 62,348,224 would be awkward to memorize as "sixty-two million, three hundred forty-eight thousand, two hundred twenty-four." Try breaking it into pieces, like *623* and *48224*. Think of the pieces as the final scores of a soccer game and a football game. Hear the loudspeaker booming "6 to 3" and "48 to 24." You'll easily remember *6 2 3* and *48 2 24*.

Memory tricks are great fun and very helpful when you absolutely, positively must know something by heart.

One Bite at a Time

Doing some heavy-duty memorizing? Spread it out over several 20-minute sessions rather than cramming it into one study marathon. Give your brain a chance to digest one set of facts before you try to pack in more.

A⁺ Mini-Quiz

Name seven super memory tricks.

_____

_____

_____

_____

_____

_____

_____

Study Wisely for Tests

Your final grade is often based on how well you take tests, so it pays to prepare for tests with extra study. If you've attended all your classes and kept up with your homework, you can usually start preparing a day or two ahead of time. You need time to review all your material two to five times. With experience you can judge how long this takes for each class.

As test time approaches, put your best study habits to use as described in chapter 2. Gather all your class notes, textbooks, homework assignments, previous tests, and handouts. Then head for your study zone and follow these steps:

1. **Review your handwritten class notes.** These are your best source of study material. They will contain most of the answers to the test questions. They should also refer to outside readings, problems, handouts, and other important materials that you need to review. If you've recorded key words, your own test questions, and main points in the left column of your notes, this now serves as a handy checklist of what to study. Note especially what the teacher told you about the test on the last day of class.

2. **Review your textbook.** You should not need to reread it at this point. Simply review the highlighted passages or your written notes about the reading.

3. **Review your homework problems until you feel happy with your ability to solve each one.** Similar problems will surely appear on the test. The key to succeeding on a math test is to be proficient in every type of problem that might appear on the test. This might seem odd, but there isn't time for thinking on a math test. You can't afford to waste time thinking about which procedures are required. You have to be able to recognize the type of problem immediately. The best way to prepare for a math test, then, is through rigorous practice.

4. **Review your previous tests from the same class to see the types of questions likely to be on the upcoming test.** Students who have taken the class before with that teacher are also good sources. They may have old tests that you can use for self-quizzing. (Just don't expect the exact same questions on your test. Good teachers vary their tests from year to year.)

5. **Make a mind map of what you have learned so far.** You might be surprised at how much you already know, and that will build your confidence.

6. **Look over all your study materials and think about what you could extract from them to organize the facts for learning.** Make lists of key terms. Draw diagrams to show relationships. Prepare flash cards for special terms or concepts you need to memorize. Group the subject into logical chunks that you can study.

7. **Now for the most important step: Working with one chunk at a time, make up your own test questions.** Study the answers as if you had to teach this subject to your younger sister tomorrow. Buckle down and apply the techniques you learned in this chapter to commit the answers to memory.

You have a wide variety of memory tricks and guidelines to choose from. Use the ones that work best for you, and watch your grades improve.

A⁺ Mini-Quiz

What are the seven steps for studying for tests?

_____

_____

_____

_____

_____

_____

_____

Which Memory Tools Will You Use?

Which memory tools will be useful in your pursuit of a better grade in your chosen subject? List them here. Also write a plan for how you will study for the next test in that class.

_____

_____

_____

_____

_____

_____

_____

_____

David

David had the soul of a poet. His mind was always off in the clouds, making pictures with words, making words sing, creating new words, and scribbling fancy words on his notebook. How could his free spirit be harnessed to the dull task of studying for the physics final?

Physics seemed so full of laws and limits. So full of dry facts to memorize. So full of formulas, forces, particles. So full of thermodynamics, velocity, vaporization, momentum, expansion, impedance, polarization…. Hey wait a minute! thought David. Physics is full of wonderful words! I could play with them!

As David studied away into the night, he committed fact after fact to memory in his own creative way—poetry. For example:

Old Newton had a notion
He called it the Third Law of Motion
For every single action,
There's an equal and opposite reaction.

(continues)

(continued)

Several chapters later he was still at it:

I speak of a force called cohesion
A molecular sort of attraction
With molecules same, that's the name of the game.
If they differ, the force is adhesion.

Yes, it was mostly bad poetry, but the rhythms and rhymes carried the physics facts quite nicely into David's brain. By the time he made them rhyme, he owned those facts. And he did quite nicely on the exam, too.

Quiz

1. Name ten ways to prepare your brain to remember a new idea.

_____

_____

_____

_____

_____

_____

_____

_____

_____

_____

2. How are your senses involved in remembering things? _____

_____

_____

3. What is the principle behind flash cards? _____

_____

_____

4. To make subjects more real, look at them from the _____ rather than the outside.

5. How can you turn a 10-minute wait into quality study time?

   _____

   _____

6. Develop a mnemonic to remember how to pronounce *mnemonics*.

   _____

   _____

7. Memory tricks are based on unusual ways to _____ one thought with another.

8. What makes brain cartoons easy to remember? _____

   _____

   _____

9. Describe how you might use a mental walk-through of your house or apartment to remember things in order. _____

   _____

   _____

10. The "peg" system is based on linking mental pictures with _____-alike numbers.

11. Creative sentences for memorizing are built using the first _____ of the items you want to remember.

12. List four things to review when studying for tests. _____

   _____

   _____

   _____

   _____

13. Lists, flash cards, and diagrams extracted from your review materials help you group the subject into logical _____ for studying.

14. Explain why making up your own test questions is a useful study technique. _____

_____

_____

True or False?

15. Practicing a procedure has nothing to do with understanding it. T F

16. Rhythm and rhyme are best avoided when memorizing important test material. T F

17. Cramming is the most effective way to prepare for a test. T F

CHAPTER 7

Tackle Tests with Confidence

You have taken extensive notes, faithfully reviewed them, and stored all the answers to your made-up questions neatly in your brain. You're now ready to unlock the final skill that leads to your success in school: mastering the art of taking tests.

Doing well on tests takes creativity and strategy. Often, it's not what you know, but how well you take tests that decides your final grade in the class. A test doesn't necessarily reflect how smart you are or even how much you know about the subject matter. It does say something about how well you take tests, though.

This chapter will prepare you for test-taking battle by showing how questions are designed and the best way to attack each type. It also arms you with good test-taking habits and strategies.

Know the Testing Techniques

The teacher has spent weeks trying to help you pack a pile of information carefully into your memory warehouse. Now he or she has crafted a series of questions to make you haul it all out again.

Making up a good test is not that easy. You can bet the teacher has to learn the subject pretty well to make up good questions. (That's why in chapter 6 we suggested you make up your own questions while you study.)

Quiz Kid?

Are you an "expert" on something? Batting averages in the major leagues? Marvel Comics characters? Soap opera trivia? Heavy metal bands and tunes? Classic automobiles? Stephen King novels? Computers?

When you know a lot about something, isn't it kind of fun to be asked questions about it? Do you sometimes enjoy watching quiz shows and trying not to be *The Weakest Link*? Do you ever get together with similarly minded friends and quiz each other?

See if you can capture that same spirit of challenging yourself on your next test. You'll see a whole different way of relating to the testing situation. The test will be more like a game, and you'll be the winner.

The reason your teacher goes to all this trouble is to check on the status of your knowledge. A test helps the teacher know what you've learned so that he or she knows what to emphasize in future lectures. It helps you know what you need to study harder to understand more clearly. A test is not supposed to be a battle between you and the teacher to see who can outsmart whom. But it does require a fighting spirit to overcome the normal test anxiety and deliver your very best performance.

To master the art of test-taking, start by understanding the methods teachers use to test your knowledge. Different types of test questions require you to use different skills. Each type gives you a slightly different opportunity to show how well you have prepared for the test.

Some ask you to recognize a correct answer. Some ask you to pull a fact out of your head. Others ask you to analyze a problem and devise a solution strategy. And still others ask you to assemble a set of ideas into a logical written answer.

Here are some hints about how to approach different types of test questions, both in studying for them and in answering them on test day.

True/False

True/false questions require that you recognize a fact or idea, but they often check whether you understand it in exact detail. If any detail is false, the whole answer is false. Watch for words that suggest that anything happens in only one way: *always* and *never*. Questions that contain these words are usually false. Also pay close attention to qualifying words such as *all, most, usually,* or *rarely.* Here's an example of true/false test questions:

Circle T for True or F for False:

T F 1. Britney Spears was born in France.

T F 2. Mozart never appeared in public because he was embarrassed to be seen in tights.

Multiple Choice

Multiple-choice questions require you to recognize a correct answer among several options. You might recognize this as the type of question asked on *Who Wants to Be a Millionaire.* They can be tricky if the choices are very close to each other in meaning. But this type of question is easier than a lot of other question types because the correct answer is right in front of you. You just have to figure out which one it is.

To avoid confusing yourself, try to answer the question first without looking at the options. Then read each option carefully. If you don't recognize the correct choice right away, see whether you can eliminate at least one or two obviously incorrect choices. Then choose the best of the remaining two. And no, you can't phone a friend.

Here's an example of multiple-choice test questions:

Circle the letter beside the most appropriate choice.

1. The 42nd president of the United States started his career as a(n):

a) peanut farmer

b) Hollywood actor

c) army general

d) Fulbright scholar

2. Elizabeth Taylor's favorite color is

a) canary

b) scarlet

c) royal

d) She doesn't have a favorite

Matching

Matching questions test your recognition of things that go together. They can be like a puzzle. As you find a match for each item, cross it off the list. That narrows your choices when you're down to the last few items you're not sure of.

Here's an example of a matching question:

In the blank, write the letter of the slogan that goes best with each fast-food chain.

___ 1. McDonald's	a. Better run for the border
___ 2. Wendy's	b. Billions and billions served
___ 3. Taco Bell	c. Visit the colonel
___ 4. KFC	d. Where's the beef?

Short Answer, Fill in the Blanks

With these types of questions, you don't have choices to help you recognize the right answers. You have to retrieve the answers directly from your memory warehouse. Usually they test your recall of key terms and facts. If you committed to memory your class notes and the highlights of your reading assignments, you can probably recall the answers with ease.

Here's an example of each question type:

1. The Diamondbacks won the 2001 World Series because:

    a. _____

    b. _____

2. The last three winners of the Super Bowl were _____,
   _____, and _____.

Story Problems

Questions like this require you to analyze a problem, recognize the appropriate method for solving it, apply the method correctly, and express the answer in the correct form. Such questions are common in math and science. Prepare for them by paying close attention when the teacher works problems on the blackboard, and by doing all your homework problems.

Here's an example of a story problem:

> *Sinbad has created a computer animation that takes up 30,450,896 bytes on his 200MB hard drive. He needs to back up the files, but he has only three blank 1.44 MB disks left (Sinbad can't afford a ZIP drive or CD burner). If he compresses the files, they will take up only 56,432 bytes. How much will Sinbad spend to back up all the compressed files on floppy disks if Kmart has disks on special for $8.95 per box of 10?*

During the test, if you don't see the path to the solution right away, ask yourself the following questions:

- What exactly is the problem?
- What information is provided?
- Which information in the story is part of the solution, and which information will I not need to use?
- Can I make a diagram of this?
- What have I done before that is similar?
- What form should the answer take?

These prompts will help you notice the clues provided in the question. Notice all the clues, write them down, translate them into math symbols and sentences, and keep looking them over. This will bring the moment of insight when you recognize the path to a solution.

As you work the problem to a solution, show all the steps and calculations clearly. Even if you've made an error, you might get partial credit if your method is correct.

Discussion or Essay Questions

Questions like these ask you to pull together what you know and organize it to answer a specific question. You could just write everything you know about the subject. But your grade will be better if you write thoughtfully in response to what was asked.

Here is an example of an essay question:

"Nancy Drew mysteries gave rise to the women's liberation movement."

Evaluate this statement and give at least three reasons why you agree or disagree, citing examples from specific Nancy Drew adventures.

Here are some tips for answering this type of question on a test:

- Before plunging into writing, make a mini-outline or mind map. Jot down the main ideas you plan to include, plus supporting details. Put the ideas in logical order. See whether they really answer the question. By doing this brief preparation, your answer will hang together much better.

  intro: agree with statement
  main points of women's lib
  　　　end powerlessness
  　　　define own destiny w/o men
  　　　actively pursue goals
  character of Nancy Drew (w/examples)
  　　　self-reliant
  　　　owns car
  　　　enlists help of women to solve crimes
  effect on readers
  　　　visualize another way
  　　　feel empowered
  　　　sisterhood with other N.D. readers
  conclusion: driving force behind women's lib.

- Begin your essay by rephrasing the question as an introductory statement:

  Nancy Drew mysteries, first published in 1930, provided the model for generations of women that culminated in the women's liberation movement.

- The body of your essay should build on your opening statement. It can be anywhere from one paragraph to several paragraphs long. It should give reasons for your statement and include details and examples to make your points.

- End with a concise statement that captures the overall theme of your answer and brings it to a logical close:

  Thus, embodying the very characteristics that men have long suppressed, the character of Nancy Drew stands as a beacon for the army of women, young and old, who toppled the male chauvinists in the 1970s and who continue to define their own destiny today.

- Quickly review what you wrote just to be sure your grammar and facts are correct.

- If you worry that you can't write well under pressure, take heart: Even poor writers can win points if they include the main ideas the teacher is looking for. Take advantage of the mini-outline strategy to make sure you include those main ideas in your answer. If you're not sure you got your ideas across, underline the key phrases to make them stand out.

Key Terms in Essay Questions

Certain words tend to show up often in essay questions. Here's what your teacher is really asking you to do when he or she uses one of these words:

analyze—take the subject apart and highlight the interrelationships of parts.

compare—draw out similarities between two items.

contrast—draw out the differences between two items.

critique—analyze an idea in detail and then present your judgment.

define—explain the meaning of a term or concept.

describe—give an overview and details.

(continues)

Key Terms in Essay
Questions (continued)

discuss—give reasons and details, especially about two sides of an issue.

evaluate—look at both sides of an issue and state your viewpoint, citing evidence to support your view.

explain—state why and how something happens or happened.

illustrate—give examples of how an idea works in different circumstances.

interpret—describe the subject's meaning and relate it to examples.

justify—explain why.

list—itemize a set of concepts in brief form.

outline—sketch the main points, showing the structure of the subject matter.

prove—present documented facts that support a point of view.

relate—draw connections between dissimilar ideas.

state—use precise terms to describe rules, laws, opinions, and so on.

summarize—give a concise overview that preserves the meaning.

trace—give a historical progression or development.

A⁺ Mini-Quiz

Name the seven different types of test questions discussed in this chapter:

_____

_____

_____

_____

_____

_____

_____

Develop Good Test-Taking Habits

Other than taking excellent notes, completing assignments, and studying hard for specific types of questions, what can you do to give yourself a head start on test day? Develop good test-taking habits. Here are some suggestions:

1. **Get a good night's sleep.** Don't expect your mind to deliver peak performance if you stayed up half the night cramming. You're better off resting to prepare your mind for quality thinking. Remember that a good night's sleep means seven to nine hours.

2. **Eat a healthy meal.** Inhale a bag of chips right before the test and your reward is indigestion. Instead, eat a light meal at least an hour before the test, including fruits and whole-grain breads or cereals—all excellent brain foods. You'll have energy for the task ahead.

3. **Dress up.** Take a little extra care with your appearance on test day. If you feel good about how you look, you'll stand a little taller and think a little more quickly. Relaxed and confident, you'll be more ready to concentrate on the test.

4. **Bring the needed tools.** Before you leave home, do a mental rundown of everything you need: a watch, extra pencils, erasers, a ruler, a calculator, test booklets, paper, or whatever. Having the right tools will help you focus on the test instead of scrambling around to borrow what you forgot.

5. **Arrive early.** Find a seat where you can be quiet and undisturbed, but where you can easily see and hear the teacher's test instructions. During the moments before the test, take several deep breaths and imagine yourself answering every question with ease. This step is important. It gives you a head start on all those folks who stroll in at the last minute.

6. **Avoid pretest chatter.** Students are often seen testing each other during the hour before an exam. Avoid this unsystematic last-minute cramming. It might confuse you more than help you, and you risk becoming anxious. Consult your notes only if you have a specific question. That way you implant nothing but correct information in your brain.

7. **Write carefully.** Your test sheet should reflect the same care you have shown with your behavior in class. Neatness counts. Take care to mark your answer sheet correctly, especially if you skip around between questions. That's the only way to receive full credit for each correct answer.

8. **Take mini-breaks.** Test-taking can be intense. A 20-second time-out for a yawn and stretch can do wonders to recharge your batteries and clear your mind. Rest before you get tired.

Have a Plan of Attack

Here's a five-point strategy to follow from the time you receive your test paper until after you turn it in. This strategy will help you get the highest grade possible on the test.

1. **Jot down notes and formulas.** As soon as you have written your name on the test paper, write down any important notes or formulas while they're still fresh in your memory. These notes might help you answer questions later.

2. **Read the instructions.** Test formats vary with your teacher's mood, so don't count on this test being just like the last one. Read and understand exactly what's required of you and how the test will be scored. For example, on some standardized tests, wrong answers are actually subtracted from your score; in this case, you would not want to take a chance on guessing the answers.

3. **Scan the test.** Look it over to see what kinds of questions you need to answer, noting the ones that you can do quickly and accurately. See how many points each section is worth in calculating your grade.

4. **Budget your time.** Quickly map out how many minutes you can devote to each section of the test. Put most of your time toward the sections that count the most in your final grade. If three essay questions together are worth 75 points on a 100-point test, don't spend more than one-quarter of your time on the remaining questions. You need time to answer all the questions if you intend to get a good grade. If you do run short of time, jot down at least the main points of your essay, with an explanation to the teacher such as "I ran out of time." If your points are

good and the teacher believes you are sincere, you might earn partial credit.

5. **Answer the simple questions first.** True/false, multiple-choice, matching, fill-in-the-blank, and short-answer questions can usually be answered quickly. Tackle these first to build momentum and increase your confidence. (But watch out! Don't work so fast that you fail to read these questions carefully.)

6. **Answer the remaining questions.** Start from the beginning and work your way to the end. This technique helps you avoid skipping questions. If you must skip one because you don't know the answer, put a check mark next to it so that you can return to it quickly later. As you continue through the test, you might think of clues to help answer the questions you skipped. In some cases the correct answers are revealed in other test questions.

7. **Read questions carefully.** Don't decide on an answer until you've read the entire question. This is a common mistake. People tend to see what they expect to see, when what's really there is slightly different. Take a closer look before drawing any conclusions.

8. **Ask for clarification.** If you truly don't understand a question, ask the teacher to rephrase it for you. But speak only to the teacher. Otherwise, you might be accused of cheating.

9. **Don't second-guess your answers.** You'll improve your chances for high grades if you avoid looking at the pattern of previous answers on your answer sheet. If you do see a pattern (A, A, B, B, C, C, and so on), don't be fooled into making any changes. You'll do much better if you respond based on what you know about the subject. If you start to doubt one of your answers, but you're not absolutely sure it's wrong, don't change it. Studies show that your first hunch is often the correct one.

10. **Be creative.** Sometimes the solution to a problem is not obvious. This can happen even if you're well prepared. In this case, relax and let your mind wander back over all your notes and homework problems. Use your imagination to create links between this tough problem and what you've been studying. Draw a picture to help you think it through. Chances are, you'll stumble on a clue that will lead you to a solution.

11. **Include details.** Load your answers with relevant facts. These show how well you understand the subject matter and earn you maximum credit. If an essay question has you baffled, try writing as many relevant details as you can, even if they do not add up to the answer that the teacher was looking for. Some teachers will give you points for showing that you know a lot about the subject. Others will take off points for citing facts that don't contribute to the desired answer, so you'll have to use your judgment. Above all, avoid trying to fake your way to an answer. Teachers can easily spot vague answers that anyone could write without ever taking the class.

12. **Have reasons for each answer.** Ask yourself how you know each answer is correct. This builds your confidence and helps later if you dispute the way a teacher graded your answer. If you can give a convincing argument for how you arrived at your answer, you might get those points added back to your score.

13. **If you're stumped, don't panic.** Breathe normally and let your mind float outside of yourself for a moment. This detaches your mind from the panic. It shuts up that little inner voice that's predicting doom and gloom for your entire future based on the results of this test. All that matters is what's happening right here, right now. After all, it's only a test, not a matter of life and death.

14. **Review the test.** If you have time left over, take a few moments to relax and clear your mind. Then review your test one more time. Reread the test instructions. Start at the beginning and work your way through to the end, checking each answer. Make sure you have shown all your work and written each answer neatly. There's no shame in being the last student to finish. Use every available minute to perfect your work, and don't hand it in until you're convinced you've done your best.

15. **Reward yourself.** When the test is over, celebrate! Treat yourself to watching a video, having a special meal, or playing your favorite sport. The goal is to link studying and test-taking with a little fun. You'll look forward to studying for future tests and the good times that follow.

A⁺   Mini-Quiz

Name the five good test-taking habits you can learn from this chapter:

_____

_____

_____

_____

_____

Review Your Results

When you get your test score back, take a few moments to bask in the glory of your victory. You followed your strategy, and now maybe there's a big, juicy *A* on your paper. Enjoy the warm feeling of success. It's a feeling you'll want to experience again and again.

To make sure you do, pay careful attention to the lecture just after the test. The teacher might review questions, and those may appear on future tests, such as a final exam. Get them all down in your notes, whether you got them right or wrong on the test. This post-test review lets you know what material your teacher feels is important. When you know that, it's easy to review for upcoming tests.

Learn from Your Mistakes

What if you didn't get an *A* on the test? The first thing you need to do is think positive! Don't compare your grade to what other students got. Rather, focus on your past successes and remind yourself that you have other successes to look forward to.

When you're over the initial shock and have regained a positive attitude, follow these five steps to move closer to your goal of high grades:

1. **Check for grading errors.** Teachers, being human, sometimes make mistakes. They might even write a clinker question that really has two correct answers. You might be able to improve your score if you can demonstrate why your answer is reasonable.

2. **Talk with your teacher.** Most teachers will go out of their way to help you, especially if you are obviously trying hard. They recognize that your learning depends in part on how well they do their job. Don't accept a low score as final until you've sorted things out with the person giving out the grades.

3. **Find a positive message.** You may feel like pitching the test in the nearest trashcan. Resist the temptation. It's easier to achieve top grades when you make a habit of gaining from your experiences. If you missed getting an *A,* review the test (however painful it may feel) to find out where things went wrong. Were your notes not detailed enough? Did you skip the reading assignments? Did you misread a problem? Did you overlook important test instructions? On essay questions, pay attention to the teacher's written comments. If you have the courage to review your test, you have what it takes to get a better grade next time.

4. **Vow to do better.** If your score is not up to your standards, make up your mind to improve it on the next test. One low grade is not a disaster. You can often revise your strategy and raise your future scores to the levels you are hoping for.

5. **Attend a "help session."** There are often help sessions available to students during, or sometimes after, the school day. These are often led by other students, who can sometimes explain things differently than a teacher might. These are free and worth the time and effort to attend.

What Will Your Next Test Be Like?

What types of questions appear on tests in your chosen subject? Which suggestions in this chapter apply to those types of questions? List the techniques you plan to try on your next test in this subject.

_____

_____

_____

_____

_____

Latanya

Latanya had her reasons to be nervous about the French exam. Her family had faced several moves recently because of plant closings, and here she was at a brand-new school in mid-December, facing a test tomorrow with a brand-new teacher, in the subject she loved best. Super conscientious, Latanya was eager to do well, but she knew that occasionally her over-eagerness played havoc with her mind during tests.

Earlier this fall, at the school she used to attend, her mind had gone blank for a few minutes when she stumbled over a verb she was supposed to conjugate. She managed to pull through, but she felt humiliated at the less-than-stellar grade that she got on that test.

Latanya shuddered thinking back on that experience. She knew it would take an effort of will to overcome her test anxiety this time. She reminded herself that this was only a test, not a measure of her self-worth. But she knew she needed more than reassurance to get her through this difficult trial. If she lost ground in school, especially in her favorite subject, it would just be more bad news for her family, and they had had enough trouble already to last the decade.

"Latanya," she said to herself, "you can do this! You have memorized the vocabulary words. You have practiced using them in all kinds of sentences. You have recited them to yourself out loud so you know how they sound. You know the grammar rules backwards and forwards. There's no objective reason for you to fear this test."

(continues)

(continued)

But Latanya's conversation with herself didn't stop there. "I seem to recall that last time you had a French test, you took your flair for languages for granted and didn't study until the last minute. In fact, weren't you looking at some parts of the French text *for the first time* the night before the test? And don't I recall that you confused yourself at the last minute by shooting grammar questions back and forth with a friend? Maybe you can avoid those pitfalls this time. In fact, I challenge you to think of all the ways you can feel prepared and confident for this test!"

Latanya's brow wrinkled as she thought about this a few moments. One final time she reviewed all her vocabulary words and conjugations. Then, with a grand gesture, she closed her French text and her notebook and put them away in her book bag. She tucked two freshly sharpened pencils alongside them. She set out her best jeans and her new turquoise sweater to wear in the morning. As Latanya brushed her teeth, she hummed a little French lullaby that her grandmother had sung to her as a child. She set her alarm clock a few minutes early and snuggled into bed.

Up at dawn, Latanya took a little extra care with her hair and makeup and surprised her parents by joining them at the breakfast table. She glided out the door throwing kisses. "Au revoir, mama, papa!" she called after her.

An hour later, Latanya was hard at work on the French exam. She had arrived early and cleared her mind of all distractions. She sat quietly and pictured herself effortlessly filling in each blank and flawlessly completing each sentence. "I'm going to enjoy this," she told herself. First she scanned the test and planned how much time to devote to each section. Then she was off and running.

Another hour later, and Latanya strode up to the teacher's desk to turn in her test paper. During the last five minutes, she had carefully reviewed her work, making sure it was neat and correct. The teacher's quick check confirmed that Latanya had nailed the test. "Merci, madame," said a jubilant Latanya. As Latanya left the room, the teacher thought she heard a loud whisper just outside the door..."Yes!"

Quiz

1. Your grade might be determined not by what you know, but by how well you take _____.

2. While studying, your brain stores information; while taking a test, your brain _____ information.

3. What does your teacher learn from your test result? What do you learn from your test result? _____

_____

_____

_____

_____

4. Which types of test questions require you to *recognize* facts that you have studied? _____

_____

_____

_____

5. Which types of test questions require you to *recall* facts that you have studied? _____

_____

_____

6. Which types of test questions require you to *analyze, organize,* or *synthesize* facts and ideas? _____

_____

_____

7. Before answering an essay question, jot down the main ideas in a mini-_____ or a mind _____.

8. In answering an essay question, what should your opening statement include? What should your closing statement include? _____

_____

_____

_____

_____

9. If you think you're a poor writer, what can you do to win some points on essay questions? _____

_____

_____

10. This chapter cited a 15-point strategy to use when you receive your test paper at the beginning of the test. Pick one key word from each point and develop a mnemonic (see chapter 6) to remember all 15 points.

_____

_____

_____

_____

_____

_____

_____

_____

_____

_____

_____

_____

_____

_____

11. Why is time management important when you're taking a test?

_____

_____

12. If you have trouble with a test question, what can you do to help your brain figure out the answer? _____

_____

_____

13. Why should you celebrate when a test is over? _____

_____

_____

14. What important things can you learn by reviewing a test after the teacher has graded it? _____

_____

_____

_____

True or False?

15. A good night's sleep has a better effect on test performance than all-night cramming. T F

16. Arriving for the test a minute or two late gives you an adrenaline rush that boosts your performance. T F

17. Wear your grubbies on test day so that you don't risk getting sweat stains on your good shirt. T F

18. What you eat before a test can affect your test score. T F

19. Last-minute quizzing with your friends will give you confidence for the test. T F

20. Yawning and stretching during a test recharges your batteries. T F

21. When reading test instructions, don't review them because your first reading is probably more correct. T F

CHAPTER 8

Go For It!

You've discovered the secrets of getting better grades. You've seen that it's possible to work smarter, not harder. You've developed a set of tools to use to make your schoolwork easier. You've set goals and followed your plans for getting a better grade in your chosen subject. Where do you go from here?

This chapter reviews the secrets and shows you ways you can apply them to other classes—and to anything you want out of life.

Make Our Secrets Your Secrets

Our secrets are secrets no more. You have seen how and why they work. Some of what you've read is probably not new to you. But maybe you learned other new things and tried them out. Here's a recap:

- You learned how to take control of your attitude and your time.

- You discovered how to set up a study zone and to plan your studying to take advantage of how your brain works best.

- We showed you how to set the stage for learning by practicing good listening habits and taking notes in class.

- We delved into reading skills, showing you how to preview, review, and do speed-reading.

- You discovered ways to organize long-term projects such as term papers so that you can complete them on time and make them as close to perfect as possible.

- We described memory tricks you can use when you study for tests.

- We shared effective test-taking habits and strategies for getting the highest scores.

Now a whole assortment of tools and techniques is at your disposal. What do you do with them?

First, you need to make them your own.

Put It All Together: A Super-Study Poster

Take a sheet of paper and go back through each chapter of this book. Pull out all the tools and techniques we have presented; however, write them in your own words. Record them in whatever format feels right and will help you remember them. The format could be a series of lists by chapter title, a formal outline with main heads and subheads, or a mind map of techniques grouped in the way that makes the most sense to you. As you write, you'll probably come up with your own ideas about what would help you be a better student. Add these to the sheet.

When you have written all the tools on the sheet, make up a title and write it at the top. Now neatly copy your summary sheet over to a sheet of poster board, highlighting the tools you especially want to try. Decorate your poster with color and pictures you've drawn or cut out of magazines. Then hang it on the wall in your study zone.

The poster will be your constant companion and a reminder of all the ways you can work toward better grades. And the very exercise of going through these methods to create your poster is actually good practice for your future studying.

Put Your Tool Kit to Work

Now you have a choice to make. Will you use these tools, or will you just forget about them and go back to your old, unsuccessful habits? If your choice is to use them, you have at least three options:

- Continue to use them in the subject in which you've chosen to improve your grade.

- Begin applying them to your other courses to improve your grades.

- Begin applying them to your life for reasons other than getting better grades.

Using the Tools in Other Courses

If you apply your tools in other courses, you'll soon discover how different subjects might require the use of different tools. You'll have a chance to explore some of the techniques more fully. For each course, be sure to write a plan for which tools you will use and for how long. Give yourself at least 21 days to establish new habits in those classes.

As you think about wider uses of your new tool kit, here are some tips to get the most out of your classes and help you stand out from the crowd:

- **Pick classes that interest you.** You'll do best in subjects that you are drawn to.

- **If you have a choice, pick teachers who love to teach.** Find out from classmates which teachers have star quality. In addition to inspiring you to do your best, an excellent teacher shows you how much fun learning can be. Every student should have that experience at least once in school. It sticks with you for a lifetime.

- **Get to know your teachers.** Learn what interests them and why they chose to teach. Seeing their point of view can help you get the most out of even the most boring class.

- **Ask each teacher what you need to do to earn a top grade in his or her class.** Then follow the suggestions they give you.

- **Do extra work.** If you have an opportunity to earn extra credit, run with it.

- **Please your teachers.** This doesn't mean being an apple polisher. It means playing the role of eager novice to the teacher's role of wise expert. In other words, stick with the script that we described in chapter 3.

Using the Tools for Other Reasons

Getting top grades is important in school. It's your ticket to getting awards, being accepted to your chosen college, winning your teachers' approval, and earning your family's praise. But we hope you'll agree there are other reasons for using your new tool kit besides getting good grades. Having a system for rising to challenges and for overcoming hurdles just feels good. You know you are prepared to meet just about anything life dishes out. College and your career are certain to tap those same skills. The sooner you become adept at using them, the easier everything you do will be. Working smarter, not harder, is its own reward.

Write Your Own Story

"Another lousy grade! That's the story of my life." Is this what you're telling yourself? Remember, your subconscious mind doesn't know the difference between what's really real and what you tell it is real. That's why that inner voice, your self-talk, has such power to make you feel bad or good. You can harness that power and use it to your advantage. Simply write yourself a new story.

Throughout this book, we have recounted stories of students who overcame problems with their schoolwork by applying the secrets of getting better grades: Rudy took control of his attitude and his time. Sheila organized her study environment. Milton practiced better listening habits. Greg taught himself to read more effectively. Juanita used good planning to overcome her fear of public speaking. David mastered physics through his own brand of memory trick. And Latanya adopted better habits and strategies to calm her test anxiety. What story will you write for yourself?

Your story will need the following elements:

- Specific goals or ambitions that you feel strongly about (for this year, or for five years from now).

- A central character: you, as you would like to be.

- Statements describing the "new" you in positive terms.

- A list of obstacles you might face.

© Park Avenue, an imprint of JIST Publishing, Inc.

- How you will overcome the obstacles.

- What benefits you gain by achieving your goals and ambitions.

- How you feel when you achieve them.

Write your story in the present tense, not the future tense, as if the benefits were already yours today. Here's an example:

> *I am a top student at the university, writing a senior honors thesis that reveals an important insight into how to clean up the global environment.*
>
> *I enjoy my coursework and find many ways it applies to the real world. I have developed excellent listening and note-taking habits that let me absorb new information with ease. I commit my class notes to memory and am relaxed and confident going into exams.*
>
> *My job is important to my finances, so I plan my time carefully to be sure that I don't neglect my studies.*
>
> *As a top student, I am much admired by my friends and family and have several job offers in my chosen field. I feel as though I can accomplish anything I put my mind to!*

Your own story will, of course, be much more exciting. Fill it with all the juicy details to make it real. Write it in strong terms that show your emotions. Then read your story to yourself, out loud, often. Your subconscious mind will accept it as real and will work behind the scenes to help make it come true.

Program Yourself to Succeed

Imagining the person you would like to become is half the battle. The other half is keeping the image alive and vivid enough to keep directing your actions. You can program yourself for success with these tips:

- **Post reminders.** Surround yourself with notes and pictures of your desired lifestyle and goals. Remind yourself often of what you want. This will keep your enthusiasm high, even while you're working through tough times.

- **Commit fully to your goals.** Eliminate "I'll try" from your vocabulary —it's too wishy-washy! Come right out with "I will." That says you mean it.

- **Turn setbacks into opportunities.** If you are firmly committed to your goals, there is no such thing as failure. You will make mistakes—that's a risk you take whenever you try for something worthwhile. But you can view them as chances to learn what to do better or differently next time.

- **Do what it takes.** Your goal won't happen if you sit back and wait. You need to put in the required effort and make the necessary sacrifices. You might have to give up some of your free time to keep up with your schoolwork. You might need to take extra classes to bring your math skills up to speed. You might have to study subjects you don't enjoy to graduate. It's up to you to make things happen. You're responsible for your own future.

- **Surround yourself with good models.** Learn more about people you admire and how they achieved their goals. Choose friends who share your vision and ambition. You can help each other reach for success.

- **Keep your sense of humor.** Laughter is good for the soul, so lighten up! Learn to laugh with yourself when you get too intense. Even the most serious work can be done in a spirit of good fun. Plus, you earn a bonus for keeping a positive outlook: People are drawn to a cheerful person like a magnet, so you'll get lots of social support.

- **Care enough to take care of yourself.** For your mind to give you its best, your body needs special maintenance. A variety of nutritious food, regular exercise, adequate rest, and a balanced approach to living—together these build a strong body to house a sharp mind.

- **Never give up.** If you wrote yourself a story, you've anticipated most of the obstacles and made plans for how to overcome them. So you'll have few surprises on the road to your goals. But you won't have thought of everything, so be prepared to dig in and take a stand for what you really want. Keep telling yourself, "I'm worth it! I can do it!" You are, and you can.

Savor Your Successes

In pursuing your vision, you'll encounter roadblocks, make mistakes, and even feel like a failure sometimes. But you'll also succeed now and then.

Treasure those moments of success. Take some time to enjoy them. Bask in their warmth. Let yourself feel how it feels to be successful. This is your reward for your efforts. So take your bow, smell the roses, listen to the roar of the applause. From such moments, you can take away powerful images and emotions to sustain you when you rise to your next challenge.

Quiz

What are the three ways you can use your new tool kit of skills for getting better grades? _____

_____

_____

_____

What are the six tips for getting the most out of your other classes?

_____

_____

_____

_____

_____

What six elements does your success story about yourself need?

_____

_____

_____

_____

_____

_____

What are the eight steps to programming yourself to succeed? _____

_____

_____

_____

_____

_____

_____

_____

Name the top three things you learned from this book. _____

_____

_____

_____

Web Sites for Getting Better Grades

In the past decade, the amount of information available on the Internet has exploded. Now you can access just about any type of information that you can imagine—and right from the source. Your parents' term papers were probably based on quotes they found in dusty, 10-year-old magazines. But you can have access, for example, to exciting information that NASA published yesterday!

But with all this information also comes a few problems. First and foremost, you must be able to judge whether the information you've found is from a reliable source. Lots of people put their opinions online, which means there's no guarantee that what they are saying is true. Look for "official" sites sponsored by recognized authorities. The sites in this appendix are some good examples.

Another thing to beware of is sites that try to entice you to buy a prewritten term paper. This is strictly forbidden in your teacher's eyes. If you're caught, you will fail the class. And you won't have learned the lesson the teacher was trying to teach you by giving you the assignment. Don't be tempted to do the wrong thing. Do the work yourself and learn something along the way.

Now, here are our picks for some of the best sites out there to help improve your study skills and provide sources for your research. Remember that this is just a sampling of the limitless resources that are available over the Internet. You can find more sites on your own by using the search engines listed at the end of this appendix.

Study Skills Web Sites

General

Fayetteville-Manlius Central School District: Study Skills for Middle School

www.fm.cnyric.org/eagle_Hill/bowers/main.htm

How-to-Study.com: Study Skills

www.how-to-study.com/

Open Directory: How to Study

http://dmoz.org/Reference/Education/How_To_Study/

Study Skills Self-Help Information

www.ucc.vt.edu/stydsk/stdyhlp.html

Homework

BJ Pinchbeck's Homework Helper

http://school.discovery.com/homeworkhelp/bjpinchbeck/index.html

BrainMania

www.brainmania.com

Education World: Study Skills and Homework Help

www.education-world.com/students/study/index.html

Listening Skills

How to Listen Better

www.how-to-study.com/how_to_listen_better.htm

Fact Monster Homework Center: Speaking and Listening Skills

www.factmonster.com/homework/speaklisten.html

Research Papers/Project Management

Researchpaper.com

www.researchpaper.com

ThinkQuest

www.thinkquest.org/index.html

Time Management

The Time Management Board Game

www.devpot.southcom.com.au/Students/priogam3.htm

Time Management for Middle School Students

www.angelfire.com/wa2/wabuildersclub/time.html

Time Management for High School Students

www.mtsu.edu/~studskl/tmths.html

About.com: Time Management Tips for Students

http://gradschool.about.com/cs/timemanagement/

Web Sites About School Subjects

Geography

National Geographic Kids

www.nationalgeographic.com/kids/

CIA: The World Factbook

www.odci.gov/cia/publications/factbook

History

American Memory Timeline

http://memory.loc.gov/ammem/ndlpedu/features/timeline/index.html

Histor eSearch.com

www.snowcrest.net/jmike/

Language Arts

Bartelby.com, Great Books Online

www.bartleby.com

Creative Writing for Teens

http://kidswriting.about.com/?once=true&

Glossary of Poetic Terms

http://shoga.wwa.com/~rgs/glossary.html

Learn to Write a Speech

http://learn2.com/06/0694/06941.asp

The Oxford Shakespeare

www.bartleby.com/70/

Mathematics

Ask Dr. Math

http://mathforum.org/dr.math/

HomeworkSpot.com: Middle School Math

http://homeworkspot.com/middle/math/

What Good Is Math?

www.richmond.edu/~ed344/webunits/math/home.htm

Politics and Government

Thomas, Legislative Information on the Internet

http://thomas.loc.gov

Science and Technology

How Stuff Works

www.howstuffworks.com/

Human Anatomy Online

www.innerbody.com

NASA's Planetary Fact Sheets

http://nssac.gsfc.nasa.gov/planetary/planetfact.html

Rader's Chem4Kids (Chemistry)

www.chem4kids.com/index.html

Science Fair Idea Exchange

www.halcyon.com/sciclub/cgi-pvt/scifair/guestbook

Book Summaries on the Web

Book Rags

www.bookrags.com

PinkMonkey.com

www.pinkmonkey.com

Spark Notes

www.sparknotes.com

Online Reference Resources and Tools

American Heritage Dictionary of the English Language

www.bartleby.com/61/

Bartlett's Familiar Quotations

www.bartleby.com/100/

Conversion and Calculation Center

(Online calculators, measurement conversion, time zones, currency exchange rates)

www.convertit.com/Go/ConvertIt

Encyclopaedia Britannica

www.britannica.com

American Library Association: KidsConnect

(Online help from school librarians)

www.ala.org.ICONN/AskKC.html

Libraries-Online

www.libraries-online.com/

LibrarySpot

www.libraryspot.com/

NetLingo

(A dictionary of terms for Internet, e-mail, the World Wide Web, and newsgroups)

http://netlingo.com

Online Style Manual and Dictionaries

http://linguistlist.org/style.html

Research-It: iTools

(Language tools, biographical and quotations resources, and maps)

www.itools.com/research-it/

Roget's II: The New Thesaurus

www.bartleby.com/62/

The WWW Virtual Library

http://vlib.org/

Search Engines for Further Research

AOL Search

http://search.aol.com

AltaVista

www.altavista.com

Ask Jeeves

www.askjeeves.com

Excite

www.excite.com

Google

www.google.com

HotBot

www.HotBot.com

Yahoo!

www.yahoo.com

analyze—To take the subject apart and highlight interrelationships of parts.

compare—Draw out similarities.

concept—Information that your brain uses to make sense out of other information it receives.

conscious mind—The part of your brain that processes and organizes the information it receives.

contrast—Draw out differences.

critique—Analyze an idea in detail and then present your judgment.

daily plan—A schedule of everything you need to accomplish in your day.

define—Explain the meaning.

describe—Give overview and details.

discuss—Give reasons and details, especially about two sides of an issue.

evaluate—Look at both sides of an issue and state your viewpoint, citing evidence to support your view.

explain—State why and how something happens.

freeform notes—Class notes taken by recording short paragraphs and key phrases.

goal—Something you want to accomplish.

illustrate—Give examples of how an idea works in different circumstances.

interpret—Describe the subject's meaning and relate it to examples.

justify—Explain why.

list—Itemize a set of concepts in brief form.

mind mapping—A note-taking technique that can help you capture the structure of a topic by using key phrases and positioning to show relationships.

mnemonics—Super memory tricks.

outline—Sketch the main points, showing the structure of the subject matter.

outline format—A structured note-taking system that involves writing the outline of the lecture in your notes.

plagiarism—Using an author's words or thoughts in your term paper without giving proper credit. Most teachers will fail you on the assignment if they catch plagiarism.

previewing—Mapping out reading material before you read it.

priorities—Things that are the most important to get done during the day.

processing—When your brain takes in information, examines it, and stores it where it belongs.

prove—Present documented facts that support a point of view.

relate—Draw connections between dissimilar ideas.

retrieving—When your brain takes information from storage and brings it back to you.

self-talk—Your inner voice, which gives you negative or positive messages that affect your performance and attitude.

speed reading—Reading more quickly by training your eye to see line by line rather than word by word.

state—Use precise terms to describe rules, laws, or opinions.

subconscious mind—Your memory bank that takes in information but doesn't categorize or organize it.

summarize—Give concise overview that preserves the meaning.

thesis—The main topic of a term paper, which you must either prove or disprove in your paper.

time-management—Keeping track of how you invest your time so that you can use it more wisely and accomplish more.

trace—Give a historical progression or development.

visual aids—Pictures, hands-on demonstrations, charts, summaries of main points, and dramatic recreations that you use to emphasize your points in an oral report or speech.

visualization—Imagining how you want your future to be, as a way to start making it a reality.

Index

A

abbreviations, shorthand, 49–50
About.com, 139
achieving goals, 12–15
acronyms, learning memory, 100–101
AltaVista, 143
American Heritage Dictionary Web site, 141
American Library Association Web site, 142
American Memory Timeline Web site, 139
AOL Search, 143
applying new skills in other courses, 131
Ask Dr. Math Web site, 140
Ask Jeeves, 143
asking questions, 95
assignments
    planning, 75–79
    starting, 82
    term papers, 79–85
association
    by memory, 97–100
    number-picture, 99
attendance, 54–55
attitude, 5
    changing, 5–9
    improving self-worth, 8
    self-talk, 6
    setbacks, 134
    test-taking, 109–111
    visualization, 8–9
audience, oral reports, 86

B

Bartelby.com, 140
Bartlett's Familiar Quotations Web site, 141
beat, reciting to a, 101
behavior. *See* attitude
BJ Pinchbeck's Homework Helper Web site, 138
Book Rags Web site, 141
brain cartoons, 97
BrainMania Web site, 138
breaks from studying, 30
building confidence, 104. *See also* attitude

C

capturing essence of lectures, 51–54
changing attitudes, 5–9
choosing role models, 134
CIA: The World Factbook Web site, 139
classroom skills, 37
    attendance, 54–55
    capturing essence of lectures, 51–54
    improving writing skills, 43–51
    listening habits, 40–42
    relationships with teachers, 37–40
    taking notes, 43. See also *taking notes*
commitments
    goals, 133
    making, 16–17
concentration, 29–30
confidence
    building, 104. See also *attitude*
    test-taking, 109–111

conscious minds, 23
Conversion and Calculation Center Web site, 142
Creative Writing for Teens Web site, 140
credits in term papers, 82

D

daily plans, 15–16
deadlines, 14
delivering oral reports, 87
determination, 134
developing new study habits, 130–131
diet, 134
discussion questions, 114–116
distractions, 39–40
diversifying study subjects and skills, 30
drafts of term papers, 82

E

Education World Web site, 138
Encyclopedia Britannica Web site, 142
essay questions, 114–116
essence of lectures, capturing, 51–54
establishing purpose of reading, 62
evaluating
    reading, 59–60
    term paper source materials, 80
Excite, 143
exercising
    memory, 25–27
    physically, 134

F

Fact Monster Homework Center Web site, 138

Fayetteville-Manlius Central School District Web site, 138
fill-in-the-blank questions, 112
final versions of term papers, 85
first drafts of term papers, 82
flash cards, reviewing, 94
formulas, reciting for memory, 101
freeform notes, 47

G

Glossary of Poetic Terms Web site, 140
goals, 12–15, 133. *See also* time management
Google, 143

H

habits. *See also* study habits
    attendance, 54–55
    attitude, 5–9
    listening, 40–42
    starting, 32–33
    success, 133–135
    time management, 5, 9–17
handling setbacks, 134
Histor eSearch.com, 139
homework, 29–30, 103. *See also* study habits
HomeworkSpot.com, 140
HotBot, 143
How Stuff Works Web site, 141
How to Listen Better Web site, 138
How-to-Study.com, 138
Human Anatomy Online, 141

I–J

identifying structure in text, 62–64
improving
  memory, 25–27, 96
  note-taking skills, 43–51
  project planning, 76–79
  reading skills, 71
  self-worth, 8
  study habits, 27–28
  test scores, 118–121
intelligence, types of, 24
internal dialogue, 6–8

K–L

key terms in essay questions, 115–116

Learn to Write a Speech Web site, 140
learning. *See* study habits
lectures, 47, 51–54
Libraries-Online, 142
LibrarySpot Web site, 142
life experiences, applying to study
  habits, 31
listening. *See also* taking notes
  habits, 40–42
  lectures, 51–52
  skills, 37
locations
  for reading, 61
  for studying, 28–29

M

making commitments, 16–17
matching questions, 112
mathematics, reading, 66–67

memory, 91. *See also* reviewing
  acronyms, 100–101
  by association, 97–100
  brain cartoons, 97
  exercising, 25–27
  improving, 96
  number games, 99–102
  recalling reading, 70–71
  rhyming verses, 101
  sentences to improve, 100–101
mind mapping, taking notes, 48
mistakes, learning from, 121–122
motivation, 5–9. *See also* attitude
multiple-choice tests, 111–112

N

NASA's Planetary Fact Sheets Web site, 141
National Geographic Kids Web site, 139
negative attitudes, 8. *See also* attitude
NetLingo Web site, 142
notes. *See* taking notes
number-picture association, 99–102

O

Online Style Manual and Dictionaries, 142
Open Directory: How to Study, 138
oral reports, 75, 85–87
organization
  identifying structure in text, 62–64
  notes, 43
  planning term papers, 79–83
  reviewing, 92–93, 104
outlines
  taking notes, 46
  term papers, 83
The Oxford Shakespeare Web site, 140

P

papers
  term papers, 75–85
  writing, 75
participation in the classroom, 37–40
pegs, number-picture association, 99
personal digital assistant (PDA), 10
picking term paper topics, 79–80
picture association, 99
PinkMonkey.com, 141
plagiarism, 82
planning, 16–17. *See also* time management
  assignments, 75–79
  daily plans, 15–16
  study time, 10–12
  term papers, 79–83
positive attitudes, 6. *See also* attitude
practicing
  listening, 41
  oral reports, 86–87
  reviewing, 93–95
  term paper source cards, 81
presentations, 75. *See also* oral reports
previewing text, 61–65
previous tests, reviewing, 104
problems, homework. *See* assignments;
  homework
projects. *See* assignments
purpose of reading, establishing, 62
Pythagorean theorem, 25–27

Q–R

questions, types of, 95, 111–116

Rader's Chem4Kids Web site, 141
reading, 59
  asking questions/guessing answers, 64–65
  evaluating, 59–60
  locations, 61
  mathematics, 66–67
  notes, 45
  previewing text, 61–65
  recall, 70–71
  speed, 65–70
  term papers, 84–85
  time management, 65
realistic goals, 14
reciting formulas for memory, 101
relationships with teachers, 37–40
reminders of goals, 133
repetition, reviewing, 95
Research-It: iTools Web site, 142
researching term papers, 80–82
Researchpaper.com, 139
reviewing, 91
  organizing, 92–93
  practicing, 93–95
  tests, 103–104, 121
rhyming verses, 101
Roget's II Web site, 142
role models, 134

S

saving teacher's notes, 45
schedules, 10–12. *See also* time management
Science Fair Idea Exchange Web site, 141
self-talk, 6–8
self-worth, improving, 8
sentences to improve memory, 100–101
setbacks, handling, 134
setting goals, 12–15
short-answer questions, 112
shorthand, 45, 49–50. *See also* writing skills
  changing attitudes, 5–8
  classroom. See classroom skills

concentration, 29–30
developing new study habits, 130–131
listening, 37
organization, 43
reading. See reading
setting goals, 12–15
taking notes, 37
test-taking, 109–111
time management, 5
visualization, 8–9
source cards, preparing, 81
source materials, evaluating, 80
Spark Notes Web site, 141
speeches, 85. See also oral reports
speed reading, 66–70
starting
new habits, 32–33
term papers, 82
stories, writing, 132–133
story problems, 113
strategies for tests, 118–121
structures
identifying in text, 62–64
outlines, 83
term papers, 82
study habits
breaks, 30
concentration, 29–30
developing new, 130–131
exercising memory, 25–27
flash cards, 94
improving, 27–28
life experiences, 31
location, 28–29
mixing up subjects, 30
reviewing, 94. See also reviewing
starting new habits, 32–33
taking notes. See taking notes
tests, 103–104, 117

time management, 29
visualization, 31
Study Skills Web site, 138
study time, planning, 10–12
styles
taking notes, 44
term papers, 84–85
subconscious mind, 23
subjects, mixing up when studying, 30
success
creating habits of, 133–135
improving attitudes, 5–9
symbols, shorthand, 49–50

T–U

taking notes, 37, 42
freeform, 47
improving skills, 43–51
lectures, 51–54
legibly, 45
mind mapping, 48
organization, 43
outlines, 46
planning assignments, 76–77
preparing term paper source cards, 81
reading, 45
reviewing, 103
saving teacher's notes, 45
shorthand, 45, 49–50
styles, 44
teachers
listening to lectures, 51–52
relationships with, 37–40
saving notes, 45
term papers, 79–85
tests
building confidence, 109–111
discussion questions, 114–116

essay questions, *114–116*
fill-in-the-blank questions, *112*
improving memory, *96*
matching questions, *112*
multiple choice, *111–112*
reviewing, *121*
short-answer questions, *112*
story problems, *113*
strategies, *118–121*
study habits, *103–104, 117–118*
true/false tests, *111*
types of, *111–116*
text. *See also* reading
    identifying structures, *62–64*
    previewing, *61–65*
    reviewing, *103*
ThinkQuest Web site, 139
Thomas, Legislative Information on the Internet, 140
time management, 5, 9–10
    daily plans, *15–16*
    mapping schedules, *10–12*
    planning, *16–17*
    reading, *65*
    reviewing, *104*
    studying, *29*
Time Management Board Game Web site, 139
Time Management for High School Students Web site, 139
Time Management for Middle School Students Web site, 139
tools, memory. *See* memory
topics, picking for term papers, 79–80

tracking, 10–12
true/false tests, 111
types of
    intelligence, *24*
    reading, *60*
    tests, *111–116*

V

verses to improve memory, 101
visual aids for
    lectures, *52–53*
    oral reports, *86*
visualization, 8–9
    planning assignments, *76–77*
    study habits, *31*
    success, *133–135*

W–Z

What Good Is Math? Web site, 140
writing
    goals, *12–15*
    legibly, *45*
    papers, *75*
    personal stories, *132–133*
    shorthand, *49–50*
    term papers, *79*
The WWW Virtual Library Web site, 142

Yahoo!, 143

zones, study. *See* locations